An Honest Trade

An Honest Trade

Booksellers and Bookselling in Scotland

Edited by

Alistair McCleery,
David Finkelstein and Jennie Renton

Foreword by Hugh Andrew

JOHN DONALD

In association with
SAPPHIRE: Scottish Archive of Print and
Publishing History Records

First published in Great Britain in 2009 by
John Donald, an imprint of Birlinn Ltd

West Newington House
10 Newington Road
Edinburgh
EH9 1QS

www.birlinn.co.uk

ISBN 10: 0 85976 673 X
ISBN 13: 978 085976 673 9

British Library Cataloguing-in-Publication Data
A catalogue record for this book is
available from the British Library

Typeset by Hewer Text UK Ltd, Edinburgh
Printed and bound in Britain by Bell and Bain Ltd, Glasgow

Contents

Foreword *Hugh Andrew*   vii
Preface   xi
Introduction *Alistair McCleery*   xiii
Biographies   xxiii

Robert Clow   1
Willie Anderson   37
Ainslie Thin   55
Bill Bauermeister   78
William Kay   96
James Glover   107
Robert Henderson   117
Margaret Squires   137

Foreword

My first experience of working in the book trade came in the winter of 1985. Somehow or other I had heard of a vacancy as Manager in James Thin's bookshop in Buccleuch Street in Edinburgh. I spruced myself up and presented myself – nervous, but prepared – for an interview. It was well after 3 p.m. and I was ushered into a room where sitting eating his lunch was a man with extraordinary piercing eyes and a shock of wiry and clearly little-disciplined hair. The interview lasted approximately five minutes before it was decided that I was suitable for the job. There followed a rapid-fire deluge of information which I barely absorbed. I walked out of the room somewhat shellshocked having had my first experience of the extraordinary Mr Jimmy. I spent almost three years at Thin's and came to realise that at its heart it was as much a great sprawling family as a bookshop. I came to understand the ethos of not simply knowing your customers but being friends with them in a shared passion for the written word. And I also met a range of characters and personalities the likes of whom I have rarely encountered since. In a corporate world these eccentricities and oddities would be ruthlessly expunged but in Thin's they were celebrated and they were part of what made the company. There was the wonderful Joyce, whose outrageous comments to customers and constant commentaries on everyday life as it passed by the window had both me and those in the shop helpless with laughter. There were the ladies of the Penguin Room, Louie in Schools, Sheila orchestrating things from the telephone room, the ever harassed but astonishingly knowledgeable Alan in Academic. But above all there was a warmth which made Thin's a shop that people were drawn to from across the world. Working there taught me lessons I have never forgotten and I hope never do. Those were my experiences in one bookshop and I am sure many who worked in the book trade at that time could replicate them in different towns and different bookshops.

But this was the 1980s, and where Tim Waterstone forged the way others were following: new bookchains sprouted up across the land, taking bookselling onto the High Street. For older-style booksellers the challenge was steadily growing and, while the new-style bookselling rarely made a profit, it proved masterly at selling the concept of profit tomorrow. Many family businesses w ere swallowed up in the corporate desire for endless growth.Õ But it was to be another hammer blow which was to see the last of the family businesses fall. In the late 1990s the collapse of the Net Book Agreement in pursuit of short-term gain caused an unrestricted price war in the world of books. It also saw new and powerful players enter the scene – the supermarkets. New technology posed another problem with the arrival of internet bookselling. In January 2002 James Thin's itself went into administration, brought down by tidal waves of change and an inability to match the terms that its bigger competitors could access. With its passing something of Scotland died. And it was the harbinger of the steady erosion of diversity and community which has turned our towns into bland replicas of each other. Ironically, the devourers of Thin's were devoured themselves and, as we enter a new and bleaker economic world, it is worth reflecting on what has been lost. Firstly, diversity and competition – the diversity and plethora of wholesalers, library suppliers and bookshops which once covered the landscape has been reduced to a few corporate giants. Monopoly has replaced choice. Secondly, history – too late we have realised the nexus of traditions and history which made these shops part of a sense of place, and too late we have realised what this loss means. And thirdly, values – values that have been replaced by the sole issue of price. Now that the orgy of retail gluttony which characterised the turn of the millennium is of necessity receding, perhaps we will be driven to reflect on what kept companies such as James Thin's trading profitably and successfully through the centuries. And perhaps a new generation will rebuild those traditions and that ethos which we have so carelessly and foolishly allowed to be trampled underfoot in pursuit of a mirage.

A priest remarked to a medieval bishop of Salisbury that the men of those days were but dwarves compared to the ancients. The bishop retorted that, while they were indeed dwarves, they stood on the shoulders of those giants. It is the giants of bookselling and their golden age which this book celebrates.

Hugh Andrew

Preface

*A*N *Honest Trade: Booksellers and Bookselling in Scotland* was an initiative of the Scottish Archive of Print and Publishing History Records (SAPPHIRE). SAPPHIRE aims to capture the social, economic and cultural history of the Scottish book trades – printing, publishing, bookselling – in the twentieth century and to document aspects of the working lives of people who have been employed within those trades and witnessed the changes that have taken place there. SAPPHIRE is a collaborative venture between Napier University and Queen Margaret University, both based in Edinburgh; SAPPHIRE also works in collaboration with a number of other universities in the UK and overseas, with organisations active in oral history, with the printing and publishing industry, and with heritage institutions. The recordings, photographs, films and ephemera gathered from a number of projects form the SAPPHIRE archive held at Napier University; this archive has provided, in turn, the material for exhibitions, publications and learning resource packs for schools. Further details can be found on our website at www.sapphire.ac.uk.

We wish to record our immense debt of gratitude to all the former members of the book trade who kindly shared their memories of life and work in Scottish book-shops and provided invaluable advice and guidance that helped to shape the project. We would like to single out Willie Anderson, Bill Bauermeister, Robert Clow, James Glover, Robert Henderson, William Kay, Margaret Squires and Ainslie Thin, who set aside considerable time to assist with the compilation of this volume. We would like to thank all those who donated photographs for their kind permission to use them. A much larger collection has been digitised for the SAPPHIRE archive than the selection we have been able to use in this book.

We would also like to thank the members of the SAPPHIRE advisory panel for their counsel and encouragement during the development and implementation of the project. The staff at Birlinn, particularly Hugh Andrew, the publisher, have taken a keen interest in the development of the book, as well as lending their considerable expertise to its production. Colleagues at Napier University and Queen Margaret University were ever cooperative and concerned for the success of the project. Sarah Bromage, in particular, was a pillar of strength in the last stages of the preparation of this book. Finally, this project has only been made possible by the generous financial support of the Edinburgh Booksellers' Society and the Scottish Centre for the Book at Napier University.

Alistair McCleery
David Finkelstein
Jennie Renton

Introduction

IN 1890 Macmillan published *The Principles of Economics* by Alfred Marshall. While the book was itself an important contribution to the 'dismal science', it also carried a key significance for publishing and bookselling in the UK for the following 100 years. It was the first 'net' book, that is, to be sold at a price predetermined by the publisher that all booksellers would agree not to discount. Macmillan was initially the only publisher to pursue this method of creating a level of predictability and stability within the book market. As others joined, the system became a cooperative movement rather than a multilateral contract signed at the one date. At a meeting in January 1895, held at Stationers' Hall in London, the booksellers came together to form the Booksellers Association of Great Britain and Ireland (the BA). One of the first resolutions put before the new organisation asked for approval of the net system of publishing and selling books: it was passed unanimously. A further meeting in October 1895 at Anderton's Hotel in London led to the formation of the Publishers' Association of Great Britain and Ireland (the PA). Trade body could now speak unto trade body; acronym unto acronym. Eventually, a refined version of the Macmillan initiative set out by the PA was agreed by the BA on Friday 24 February 1899. This was the Net Book

Agreement (NBA) that held sway for most of the working lives of the interviewees represented in this book. The NBA was celebrated at a dinner in May 1901, presided over by Frederick Macmillan; the attendance of 300–400 members of the trade – publishers, booksellers and indeed authors – demonstrated the consensual nature of the scheme now applying throughout the UK.

Not that there had always been the need for two trade bodies or an agreement between them. It was not until the nineteenth century that the distinction between booksellers and publishers was by and large complete. (The combination of printers and publishers was to persist into the twentieth century.) It had only been in the fifty years or so before 1890 that, instead of printing and publishing the books that they sold in their shops, booksellers largely bought their stock directly from the publishers. This of course had created a conflict: publishers wanted to sell their books at the highest price possible; booksellers wanted to buy cheaply and sell to make a profit. Throughout the nineteenth century, booksellers encountered serious problems in keeping their profit margins high enough to be viable. At an early stage, booksellers realised that their survival lay in convincing the publishers to give them favourable terms and discounts in order to secure both their profits and cashflow. The solution was obvious to the booksellers: the publisher would fix a retail price, allowing the books to be sold to the bookseller at a discount. The problem was to convince publishers that it would work. A first attempt was made in 1829 when publishers and booksellers drew up the Bookselling Regulations, which sought to fix trade and retail prices for books. However, these regulations were not universally accepted and the agreement, forerunner of the NBA, broke down in the late 1830s. This was the era of 'free trade', when the general political mood was against price fixing of any sort. It was difficult for booksellers to find champions of their idea for a fixed retail price for books, both within the trade and outwith it. Booksellers continued to struggle in a very competitive marketplace, while publishers found it difficult to find outlets for their stock as more and more bookselling businesses failed. Writers suffered too. They had earlier banded together as the Society of Authors in 1883, driven by the need to protect their rights and optimise their incomes. Their representative Walter Besant had been involved in the discussions with the PA and BA and saw the NBA as a means of providing stability for authors as well as those more directly involved in the book trade. Little wonder that the NBA had been approved by all parties.

The twentieth century began then with the prospect of security and growth in bookselling; it was to end, as will be seen, in uncertainty and consolidation. There were some hiccups on the way: the so-called 'book war' of 1906–8 resulted from the establishment of a net price-discounting book club by *The Times* in 1905 (a *Glasgow Herald* book club founded in 1907 lasted only a year); the successful marketing of the sixpenny paperback by Penguin from 1935 seemed initially to challenge financial stability because of the relatively small margins on the sale of each individual title, until booksellers realised that the 'Tesco principle' of volume sales and low retail (net) prices could result in as healthy a profit as limited sales of high-priced hardbacks; and there were government-derived challenges to the general application of Retail Price Maintenance (RPM; the generic term for schemes such as the NBA) in the period after the Second World War. These challenges originated in a sense that the interests of the individual consumer were not being served by such price fixing, although the argument of the 'greater good of the greater number' – that is, of a general social benefit being produced – underpinned the survival of RPM for both books and medicines. Publishers and booksellers cared for the intellectual and imaginative health of the whole nation.

The NBA did, it must be admitted, create a complacency within the book trade that is at times represented in these interviews. While various retailing revolutions transformed the rest of the high street, the cosy (for the bookseller) and intimidating (for many readers) bookshop resisted change until the last third of the twentieth century. Indeed, the dissolution of the voluntary agreement that was the NBA in 1995 (by the publishers rather than the book-sellers) further accelerated a period of very rapid change within bookselling that shattered any remnants of compla-cency. A sense of regret and bewilderment at the speed and nature of such change is also represented in these interviews.

Bookselling had been a genteel vocation: entry was often as a result of accident or birth. Professional training was through a period of apprenticeship – partly abroad, where possible, in the major continental book centres of Paris or (pre-1939) Leipzig. Experience was gained in various departments and of the diverse functions of the trade before a position in management opened up. This relatively insular formation contributed no doubt to the general conservatism of the trade through the perpetuation of familiar (and familial) practices from generation to generation. Book-shops could not be easily distinguished from libraries; both were cathedrals of books with dim, daunting interiors that only the most confident, those who were knowledgeable of local ritual and observances, dared enter. There was little direct competition, and consequently the service to customers could be quite casual. Books not in stock could take weeks, if not months, to arrive as the result of a distribution system seemingly designed by Heath Robinson. (I write from experience of the offhand treatment of customers by staff of a monopolistic bookshop in a middling-sized town in the 1970s.) The sentimentalised image of the bookseller as a guide and mentor to good reading that still pops up in a film such as *You've Got Mail* (1998), by contrast with the efficient but soulless chain retailer, does not necessarily reflect the reality of the historical situation of the early twentieth century. It is to the credit of the generation of booksellers represented in this book that they began to initiate in the 1960s, once they gained management positions, long-overdue change.

That evolutionary change, working within independent booksellers, building up small localised chains, emerged from a context of increased disposable income and leisure time, both being intensively competed for by other media and activities. More particularly, it also emerged from the rapid expansion of higher education in the UK during the 1960s, both in the number of students going on to tertiary study and in the number of new institutions being created to cater for them. Dynamic companies like John Smith and James Thin began, for example, to computerise their stock and ordering systems, a difficult task given the non-standardised, diverse nature of the goods being sold compared to other forms of retailing. The key to many of their reforms was improving the level of service and choice offered to the customer. Those customers could be drawn into environments that were better lit, more colourful, more welcoming. As can be read in the accounts of John Smith, bookshops began to host events from musical recitals to authors' readings and signing sessions, converting the curious into regular customers. This was unprecedented – Dickens did not tour bookshops, only theatres and concert halls. (Not that there were not diehards, in the literary world who felt that a sacred product like the book needed a reverential and meditative ambience – but that, at least until the 1980s, was what libraries continued to provide.) The reform-minded bookshops offered from the 1960s a wider stock, more efficient ordering systems, helpful staff and unhurried surroundings that encouraged the customer to browse without feeling intimidated.

And yet, like the efforts of the Duma in pre-revolutionary Russia, these reforms seem at one and the same time correct and necessary in the light of prior practice and failure to adapt, but narrow and inadequate in the light of the social and commercial changes that ultimately swept away many of the independents, including the small chains. This is the miracle of retrospective vision. At the time, few would have anticipated the end of what Edward Shils called the 'bourgeois era' through Thatcherism's enthusiasm for the market, and mass participation in the market, followed by New Labour's continuing emphasis on access and participation in a broader-based civil society. These may be most easily seen in the transformation of public libraries, which moved away from books (and the bourgeoisie and aspirant working class) to provide a variety of products in surroundings, which included soft furnishings and conversation, that resembled bookshops. But it affected bookshops as well. The larger chain bookshops like Waterstone's or Borders that emerged from the 1990s onwards sold a lifestyle as much as they sold books, offering the sofas, coffee and unpressured leisure reflected in a TV series like *Friends*. The small independents and small chains that had initiated reforms now saw them taken up by these larger chains on a scale, with a degree of capitalisation and commercial clout, that they could not emulate. Some disappeared; others, such as John Smith and James Thin, were taken over by larger companies. The statistics are unavailable for Scotland, but Laura J. Miller, in her excellent *Reluctant Capitalists: Bookselling and the Culture of Consumption* (University of Chicago Press, 2006), provides comparable figures for the USA. In 1991 independents accounted for about one third of all adult books sold there, but by 1997 their share had fallen to less than a fifth. The Scottish evidence for this revolution is found on the high streets of its large conurbations and in the pages of this book.

It was also seen on the shelves of the bookshops. Where the 1960s reformers had moved towards offering customers greater choice and had supported local publishers, the chains returned to a more restricted range of titles, held in greater numbers, to give the market what it wanted. A system of central buying was, and is, practised by some of these retail chains, whereby orders are placed by a central purchasing manager generally located at head office. This has the effect of homogenising title buying, which acts against the interests of small publishers who produce only a handful of titles a year and against titles which may seem to have a Scottish appeal only. The rationale behind such a system is that less time is taken up seeing the representatives of each publisher and that the discount structures are simplified. There is anecdotal evidence, at least, to suggest that titles published in Scotland do not fare well under central buying schemes, as they come from small publishers and/or are not viewed as appropriate for a UK market. The chains argue, in their defence, that the dedicated Scottish sections of their bookshops make up for this. Those independent retailers that remain do buy smaller quantities than wholesalers and the chains, and the discounts given to them are generally lower, but their continuing presence, particularly outside the major cities, can make a difference to small publishers whose print runs are limited and whose market is distinctively Scottish. In some cases, titles may be available only through the independents, as their potential is deemed too small for either the wholesalers or chains. By the early years of the twenty-first century, the control of most Scottish retail outlets was located outside Scotland, a development seen by those within the Scottish publishing industry, as well as those concerned for the choices available to Scottish readers, as being undesirable. These vital links in the supply chain are geographically distant from the Scottish market and hold no particular remit to promote books from Scotland or to service the Scottish, as distinct from the British, reader.

There matters might have remained from that point onwards, and the close of the careers recorded in this book, but for two factors: online bookselling and the entry of the large supermarkets. By 2000, the world wide web had become an established resource for retail selling and purchasing of all sorts. It had also become a powerful tool for promoting goods of all sorts. This situation was partly due to the success of Amazon, launched as an online book-shop in 1995 with a user-friendly interface and the use of 'intelligent agents' to replace the bookshop assistant and with a range of 'stock' far outstripping any constrained by a physical building. Its founder, Jeff Bezos, was named

INTRODUCTION

Time magazine's Man of the Year in 1999 for the manner in which he had transformed online shopping. The nature of the web means that its outreach is global (although the books still have to be dispatched) and titles can be browsed online by those living in even the remotest communities in Scotland who may never have had access to a bookshop. The advent of internet bookselling has also given to publishers a more level playing field in which to sell their books. In 2005, the then Scottish Publishers' Association launched BooksfromScotland.com, an internet site that features and sells over 13,000 Scottish-interest titles.

The phenomenal online sales and massive discounting, in particular by Amazon, of titles such as the Harry Potter series weakened the chains and provided a role model for supermarkets such as Tesco. The latter realised the principle of its founder, noted above, in slashing the prices of a narrow range of titles, especially those boosted by external factors such as selection by television book clubs, and selling them in large volumes. Buying books, or at least choosing from a limited number of titles, has become for many part of the weekly shopping trip. Books remain a significant source of cultural capital as well as, for the moment, the chief medium for learning and teaching. Independent booksellers have survived, albeit in smaller numbers and in a radically altered trading environment. The principles of economics, or at least the operation of an unregulated market, ended the world of bookselling captured in the interviews in this book as much as *The Principles of Economics* had begun it.

Alistair McCleery

Biographies

ROBERT CLOW

Robert Clow was born in Xian, China, in 1934. He was sent to boarding school in Chefoo, on the north China coast, at the age of five. He was interned by the Japanese from 1940 to 1945. At the end of the war he attended Eltham College, London before undertaking national service in the RAF. His bookselling apprenticeship included spells at J. & E. Bumpus in London from 1956 to 1959 and in Geneva in 1960. He returned to John Smith & Son, Glasgow in 1961, where he remained until 1994, latterly as managing director and chairman. He now pursues his passion for architectural restoration, serving formerly as chairman of the Architectural Heritage Society of Scotland and also of the Heritage Building Preservation Trust. He is currently a part-time farmer, raising beef cattle and sheep.

WILLIE ANDERSON

Willie Anderson has worked for John Smith & Son since 1973, when he joined it from the Royal Bank of Scotland Ltd, working initially as a shop floor assistant. He was appointed to the board of the company in 1979 and became managing director in 1994. He is now deputy chairman. From 1995 to 1997 he was president of the Booksellers'

Association of Great Britain and Ireland. He is chairman of Book Tokens Ltd and a non-executive director of Edinburgh University Press. From 1989 to 1994 he sat on the management committee of the Booker Prize. He has also been a judge both for the Whitbread Literary Prize and the Macallan Short Story Competition. He was a member of the Literature Panel of the Scottish Arts Council.

AINSLIE THIN
Ainslie Thin abandoned a possible career as an industrial chemist to join the family bookselling business. He put it upon a sound commercial basis, introducing more up-to-date methods of stock management and overseeing its expansion across Scotland. He built up James Thin to the point where it was the most successful independent chain of booksellers in Scotland and had taken over another retail chain in England. He established with his cousin, Jimmy Thin, the Mercat Press for the publication and reprinting of key works of Scottish history and culture.

BILL BAUERMEISTER
Bill Bauermeister was born in 1937. He joined the family bookselling business on leaving the Royal High School in Edinburgh. As his responsibilities increased, he managed the expansion of the company's business and consolidated its presence as a prominent feature of the Edinburgh townscape in its shop on George IV Bridge. He was also one of the first booksellers in Scotland to integrate computerised stock management and purchasing systems into book sales support. Since retiring, he continues as an active member (and treasurer) of the Edinburgh Booksellers' Society. He cultivates his garden in Juniper Green with enthusiasm and expertise.

WILLIAM KAY

William Kay joined John Menzies as a young apprentice in its Glasgow wholesale branch, rising to become its assistant book manager and acting as the company's rep to booksellers throughout Scotland. A sideways promotion to Edinburgh led to his role as Menzies' main link with publishers before he moved to London as the book manager in 1966. On leaving John Menzies in 1968, he set up in business for himself, opening Kay's Bookshop in the leafy Edinburgh suburb of Morningside.

JAMES GLOVER

James Glover was born in Edinburgh in 1924. He was educated at Boroughmuir senior secondary school before service in the RAF, during which he trained as a bomber aimer. On leaving the RAF in 1946, he joined James Thin in Edinburgh. From 1959 to 1965, he acted as sales representative for Hamish Hamilton, particularly for its Phaidon Press list. In 1965 he was appointed sales manager (later becoming sales director) of Hamish Hamilton Ltd. He returned to retail bookselling in 1973 as managing director of the White Horse Bookshop, Marlborough, and later added a bookshop in Newbury and the Bell bookshop, Henley on Thames, to his responsibilities. James Glover retired from managing the White Horse bookshops in 1989.

ROBERT HENDERSON

Robert Henderson was born in 1928 in Leith, where he was also educated. He served during the Second World War in the Royal Electrical and Mechanical Engineers, where he learnt his trade as an electrician. However, he contracted TB, and on being discharged entered bookselling as a less strenuous occupation. He worked his way upwards from sweeping the floor to becoming the manager of the Edinburgh Bookshop in George Street. He joined Thomas Nelson and Sons as its Scottish rep from 1962 to 1964 before returning to the Edinburgh Bookshop. In 1975 he was appointed manager of the Grant Educational bookshops until its parent company went into liquidation in 1982, when he became manager of the Thistle Book- shops. On retiring from bookselling, he set up a successful business producing and selling burglar alarms.

MARGARET SQUIRES

Margaret Squires was born in rural Cheshire in 1939. She read philosophy, politics, and economics (PPE) at Oxford (St Hilda's College), where she met and later married Roger (New College), who taught philosophy at St Andrews University all his working life. She worked for one year at Bankers' Trust Company as an investment analyst and, after her marriage, for two years as a research assistant to David Butler on the book *Political Change in Britain*. From 1969 until her retirement in 2006 she worked in and then managed the Quarto Bookshop, St Andrews. By the time she had reached retirement, *Today's Golfer* reported that it was 'the best golf bookshop on earth'. In her 'spare time', she brought up two children, acted as secretary to the inaugural St Andrews community council for four years, took on various roles in the local Labour party, and chaired the inaugural Fife Health Council for four years. She has climbed all of the Munros, cycled from Land's End to John O'Groats with her daughter (then 14), and is attempting the Corbetts in her retirement.

Robert Clow

CAREER DECISIONS

I came into the book trade – it must have been about fifty years ago – quite by accident. I had come out of doing national service in the air force with no idea what to do next, apart from some sort of executive work, and my only aunt suggested three firms I ought to apply to. One was J. & P. Coats, one was Cadbury, and the other was Rowntree. And I asked her afterwards why it was that she had chosen those three, and she said, 'They were all founded by individuals with high Christian ideals!' I applied to all three and all three generously gave me an interview and offered a job with the prospects of getting onto one of their various management training schemes.

For the Coats interview I stayed with Jack Knox, who for some three difficult years had been my and my sister's guardian, starting when I was eleven. Both my parents had been medical missionaries and had worked out in China, where I was born, all their lives. After the war I'd been repatriated, as my older sister and I had been separated from our parents for six years. They were in Free China and our boarding school in Chefoo was in Occupied China, so after Pearl Harbour the Japanese rounded up all the non-German and -Italian foreigners, including us, and we spent the war in the Civil Assembly

Centre, a polite name for a concentration camp, outside the town of Weishein. When my sister and I came back to the UK in December 1945, our parents remained in Scotland for a month, fixed us up with one of their former friends, Jack Knox, as our legal guardian (he was then chairman and managing director of John Smith & Son, booksellers in Glasgow) and disappeared off to China again, taking with them my three brothers, whom we had just met for the first time a month earlier.

When I got back home from the three interviews, he'd sent me a letter saying that rather than going into J. & P. Coats in cotton – which had always rather intrigued me because my grandparents had been in cotton – why not become a bookseller? 'I could train you, and if you are successful, I need someone to follow me. But if you're not successful, I'll certainly let you know, and you'll not follow me.' I thought I might get much further in Coats as they had a huge operation in Glasgow and Paisley and I wanted to go abroad again, perhaps to South America this time, but in John Smith's I might end up my own boss. And I must say the latter appealed to me. And of course, now, J. & P. Coats is no longer in Glasgow or Paisley, and until about ten years ago, Smith's was going strong. Sadly, it is now owned by a Canadian company and only a shadow of its former self. However, I was lucky to make the right decision even for the wrong reason.

APPRENTICESHIP

Mr Knox suggested I spend a year in a chartered accountant's office, opposite John Smith's St Vincent Street premises, to get to know something about bookkeeping and finance. Ironically, much later Jack Knox found out that

that building had been the town house of the third John Smith! So I actually worked in his town house and used to be called by the other apprentices to watch the ladies in the accounting department of John Smith's directly across the road having a jolly good chatter, larking about and smoking when they should have been working a little harder! After a year I knew how to lick and stick on stamps, and had taken a somewhat elementary course in bookkeeping and accountancy, but had undertaken little else.

I was therefore sent down to London, to train for three years in J. & E. Bumpus under a Scotsman, J. G. Wilson, who had been undoubtedly the leading bookseller in London in the 1930s, having learnt the trade under Jack Knox's grandfather in John Smith's! It was an incredible experience in a negative sort of way. The Old Man was eighty years old. His son, also in the business, was more interested in catching book thieves. The girl who ran the art section was dismissed, as she was caught taking a book home to read without booking it out. The lady who looked after history books was permanently asleep, not always on her feet. Her friend, who kept the biography section, permanently knitted what turned out to be a one-piece green woollen dress for herself. In triumph she wore it. After the first day I noticed the hemline had descended a little. Each subsequent day it descended further, until it reached her shoes. Thereafter it never made a reappearance, and she ceased to knit. Miss Cocking (in charge of fiction) was disabled, having broken both legs, which had both been very badly set. She spent some time trying hard to dissuade me from reading Laurence Durrell's *Justine*. I had to read it with the aid of a dictionary, such was his vocabulary! 'A filthy book, a filthy book,' she exclaimed.

3

She was given permission to go home early to avoid the 5.30 p.m. rush hour. I was returning one day at 5 p.m. when I saw her at the head of the bus stop queue, using both her walking sticks on the legs of intending passengers, competing to gain the platform of the open bus. She was quite able to fight for herself when required! The head stockman, who controlled the ordering system, had served in Egypt during the war. This had left him with little love for Egyptians, and the first order I landed was for fifty medical books for a charming Egyptian doctor. It took a month to restore a reasonable relationship with the head stockman! The company was creaking in every possible way. The long lease in Oxford Street, near Marble Arch, had no provision for rent increases. The lease was about to expire, so the bookshop was currently on a peppercorn rent. The accounts were out of control, so the auditors ran the books of account, working full-time in our premises. Many of the customers were titled ladies still living in Mayfair, and the Old Man insisted on serving them himself, in his office, as walking was difficult. Although short of money, they couldn't resist the Old Man's pressure to buy, so the next day their chauffeur, or they themselves, would come in and return all the books they had just been charged for by the Old Man. Although he always saw the customers' invoices daily, he never asked to see the returns credit notes! There was no stock-checking system and every member of the staff, with very few exceptions, was a highly individualistic character and eccentric to boot – including the Old Man!

When the three years were about up, I told Jack Knox that I wished to go to America after doing three years in London. He said, 'No, don't – the American book trade is disorganised, you're much better going to

4

Europe.' I then spent six months in Geneva, but to get a work permit I had to arrange for a Swiss bookseller to work in Glasgow. I worked in the Librairie Payot, 40 rue du Marché in Geneva, as the shop's English bookseller. However, they wouldn't let me select or buy the English stock. Instead, a Polish ex-RAF pilot, who had worked in the UK during the war, had the job, so all the older titles were popular paperback war stories and memoirs, and every one of the new titles was from the Olympia Press in Paris. These consisted of paperbacks in English of titles like *Fanny Hill*, Aubrey Beardsley's erotica and virtually every other book that was banned in the UK and in Switzerland. They used to arrive in jackets from the *Teach Yourself* series and other trusted publications to avoid scrutiny by Swiss customs. Obviously the customs officers didn't bother to check the contents or question why so many copies of the *Teach Yourself* series were being imported into Geneva! As the 'new' stock arrived in my English section, it was fairly obvious that Mr Belowski had read every copy of the Olympia Press editions, several times, as his dirty finger marks clearly betrayed his literary tastes!

After six months, autumn set in. Geneva in the damp autumn is not the most exciting place to be, though it was great during the summer. Believe it or not, I was home-sick, something I never thought I would experience, so I returned to the UK. On my first day in London I realised I'd made the first great mistake of my life. I should have stayed in Switzerland for the skiing. However, I worked in the Times Bookshop under Cyril Edgeley for a while over Christmas. Andre Deutsch, at a public trade meeting, very kindly offered to take an aspiring young bookseller into

Deutsch just to show him how the other side worked. I went up to him after the meeting and said: 'Did you really mean that, Mr Deutsch?' and he said: 'Yes, of course.' So I joined Deutsch in early 1960, nominally for two weeks that stretched into two months. What's more, he paid me, which left me quite surprised.

I was systematically put through all the departments and shown everything, including the complexities of the royalty payments to George Mikes. Both combatants, Deutsch and Mikes, were Hungarian Jewish, and both tried to outmanoeuvre each other in a friendly sense of rivalry. Diana Athill and Nicholas Bentley were his other two directors: one a highly respected author in her own right, the other a brilliant cartoonist of the time. Judy Gordon Walker (first wife of Graham C. Greene of Jonathan Cape fame and daughter of a then-famous Labour politician) was his publicity girl. She let me write the sales blurb for a frothy novel called *Waiting for Julie*. For this forthcoming publication I submitted my copy, which I was sure would induce a high subscription from the booktrade. My blurb was rejected and Judy wrote another, much to my disappointment. When I went round with the Deutsch central London rep, not one bookseller bought a copy! I was disillusioned with the booktrade! However, they all ordered it up on Monday or Tuesday morning, after the Sunday papers' reviews. Andre Deutsch frequently dined with the leading newspaper book reviewers and did appear to receive an unduly high proportion of book reviews out of proportion to his volume of production. Having completed a tour of all the departments, I returned to Glasgow and joined John Smith's as assistant managing director – theoretically.

JACK KNOX

Jack Knox had been chairman and managing director since the death of his father when he was only twenty-two. He therefore had to return to Glasgow in rather a hurry, having spent a few years' training in Bumpus, like me. I don't think he really appreciated a youngster coming in and making suggestions on how the company might be changed to bring it a little more up to date. He had worked by himself for about forty years and very slowly the company had expanded, although the atmosphere in the bookshop was depressingly similar to what had obviously existed in pre-war days. It was fairly obvious that the firm was creaking, in its systems, its organisation and its finances. I started in a fairly elevated position, but really I was just another office boy working in Jack Knox's office for the first hour or two of the day. I helped him open the mail, sort it, and then I went down to the shop floor, spending the rest of day as an ordinary bookshop assistant. But after about ten years one had a pretty good view of the company and what needed to be done. The bookshop was very busy at various times of the year – school prizegivings, summer reading, return of the university, Christmas – but I can remember actually falling asleep at my desk in February and March, when there was absolutely nothing to do. Nobody came in!

Jack Knox was incredibly handsome. My mother told me that when she and her friends were girls, and later medical undergraduates, they used to go into Smith's just to see him. He was also a very keen rugby player, or rather had been, in addition to being deeply Christian, to the point that every morning he read his New Testament first thing, at work. He was also a very fair man, though I thought he was harder on me than he was on anybody else, but then . . .

As I said, every morning I would go into his office, and we'd sit and open the mail. It would then be distributed to the various departments. There were about four or five in those days, and the orders would go into departmental 'blads', or ring binders, so they wouldn't get lost, to be matched to stock. Thereafter, the mail orders and those taken in the shop went to the ordering department, where three or four typists spent all day typing up the orders in a very complex manner onto 5 x 3-inch cards, the same information four times, and then repeat the information onto orders, to be sent to the publisher. In those days, each order blad might consist of three to five orders per department. Latterly, each of the many departments on all six floors might have thirty to forty mail orders coming in each day, the volume of business had grown so much, by which time mail opening took up to an hour or an hour and a half, with several people working on the job.

When I joined, the bookshop in St Vincent Street was on only two floors: the ground floor and the basement. Jack Knox's office was on the first floor, where the girls in the accounts department also worked. He had a huge great glass-fronted mahogany bookshelf, a vast piece of furniture that stretched almost the width of his room, which he had picked up for next to nothing because of its size. It looked like a Dutch piece because of its inlay, which was slightly crude on closer examination. Apart from that, there was one filing cabinet and a rather attractive mahogany desk. He had one secretary who worked outside his office and protected him from the public, but not from *all* the staff, who throughout the year would come to see him individually and ask for an increase in salary (paid one week in advance and one week in arrears).

The amount of time spent in salary negotiation must have been extremely expensive.

It was an interesting relationship with Jack Knox. Socially I called him 'Uncle Jack', but I remember once saying to him in conversation, fairly shortly after I'd joined the company, 'What do I call you, Jack or Mr Knox?', and he said 'Mr Knox'. So it was left on a sort of formal basis if one was talking in front of other people. But as I said, I was fairly young and after working in Bumpus and Switzerland I had a pretty good idea of how not to run a bookshop, rather than how to run a successful one. Although I had a very high regard for Swiss booksellers, I had found the Geneva bookshop somewhat chaotic, and it could have done with reorganising. I therefore came back with one or two ideas of what to do, but every time I put forward an idea or a detailed memorandum for discussion or acceptance, it was turned down accompanied by the mantra, 'No, I'm not prepared to do that', and the subject was never again raised by him. Later I learnt that it was best to introduce a subject generally and gently at six o'clock, before going home, when he felt more relaxed, but still ideas were seldom accepted.

BOOKSHOP FINANCES

In those days, we had the most terrible difficulty finding sufficient money to pay the fortnightly salaries. Any member of the public who asked for credit was automatically given it, and the accounts department had thousands of accounts in the various names and addresses of any Glaswegian who wished credit. Some academics, I am sorry to say, abused the system. To complicate matters, the three shops that we owned up by the university all had their individual accounts, but doctors could not understand why they would get three or four statements from the one firm at different times of the month, all from John Smith. Some found it extremely irritating, but there was no way that staff could tell that a hospital address for one doctor might also relate to the same doctor's home address. Sometimes medics and academics would go wild with anger at this perceived incompetence and muddle!

Because we spent so much money on extending credit, and running this account system, every fortnight we had to scuttle around looking for money to pay wages. We paid a week in advance and a week in arrears. But I could not get Jack Knox to do anything about it, and in the meantime we had thirty lasses in the accounts department running the sales and purchases ledgers. A year after he retired we had four or five. For three or four months, from October to January, we were lending large sums on what was known then as the 'seven-day money market'. We also changed from paying a week in advance to paying monthly in arrears into the individuals' bank accounts. A very difficult transition period was experienced but was overcome by subbing salaries, and over several months reducing the subbing.

The order system was creaking as well, because everything was typed up four times in the most complicated manner. It was fairly obvious that if the same information was retyped four or five times, it would be simplest to use carbon paper and redesign the shop card-index system to one that could also be used to run the cross-index system and also raise an order to the publisher, all in one typing operation. So we introduced a single-copy order slip, which also provided our internal records under separate records of author, title, publisher and date, as customers frequently had no idea of when they had ordered a book, let along remember its exact title. This suggestion was put forward in detail to Jack Knox, but received the same dismissal. So for about ten years the typists ended up typing four times as much work as was really needed. Every idea that one put forward, they were all turned down, and this went on for about ten years.

FIRST RESPONSIBILITIES

One day one of the senior men who ran one of the university bookshops died very suddenly. He was a man called Ken Saville, who'd been chairman of the Booksellers' Association. His own shop had gone bankrupt because he spent too much time on BA affairs. He had joined John Smith's as a buyer and then he'd been moved up to run the small academic bookshop, called Stenhouse, that Smith's owned. He died suddenly of a heart attack just before the new academic year started. So I was asked by Jack Knox in October to go up and run this small bookshop with a staff of three, myself included, and a huge turnover. It nearly killed all of us working from 7.30 in the morning until 9 or 10 at night. I immediately understood why Mr Saville had died! I remember going up to this university bookshop and thinking I could sort out the problems of the relationships with Glasgow University in about six months.

The teaching staff at the University preferred to buy books from Blackwell's in Oxford, rather than Smith's, as our stock was so poor. They also expected a provincial university bookshop to carry the same stock as Blackwell's, not knowing that only 5 per cent of Blackwell's turnover came from Oxford. The rest came from overseas, or from universities throughout the UK, where academics didn't use their local bookshop, like Glasgow's academics. Six years later the problems had not all been solved.

These problems, apart from lack of a selection of new publications that *might* be of interest to them, centred around the supply of recommended reading information given to students at the beginning of each term, but more particularly in October. The result was that it was very difficult to purchase in advance to meet a demand that would be created by the lecturers. We also didn't know what degree of recommendation would be attached to books on the booklist. Some lists had four or five titles, and students might be encouraged to purchase one or two copies. Others were for borrowing from the library, but the bookshop might not be told this. Some lists must have confused the students, for there might be thirty titles on it with no recommendation as to which was the most useful book to purchase. Other academics refused to give us book information, saying they were not there to boost booksellers' profits. Some didn't care. Others went on holiday for three months, and when they came back they gave us the book information at the beginning of term. They gave the same information to their students, telling them they had given us the information (true) but didn't tell them it had only been given to us the day before. Then they might cover themselves by saying, 'Anyway, John Smith's won't have it in stock!' (Also true!)

We couldn't win, and we weren't helped by the publishers' inability to get books out of their warehouses at that time of year. In those days Longman took three months to get books out of Harlow up to Glasgow, including all the Oliver and Boyd stock of Gaelic textbooks. When these arrived, it was inevitably the wrong title, as Gaelic looks all the same to store-pickers in Harlow, but it took another two months to get the right title. Then we would receive their annual circular saying that they were

ROBERT CLOW

back to a three-week delivery, in late spring! In the end,
we devised a system of collecting book information in a
standard form that then related to the ordering system
and stock control, which was then starting to come into
fashion. But we could then tell the students exactly when
we received the book information, how many copies we
had sold, whether the title was on order or not, and the
same information could be given to the lecturer. The
following year we could advise the lecturer how many had
actually been sold, so when it was suggested that we must
order 100 copies, we could let a lecturer know that the
previous year we had only sold forty-five of that particular
title. All this was manually undertaken and a huge labour.

So anyway, one day Jack Knox rang me up and said:
'I'm going to retire in about a month's time, so you'd
better come down and learn the business.' I went back to
St Vincent Street in 1964/1965. By that time, I'd reor-
ganised the three shops and we'd established Stenhouse,
which until then had been a medical and academic bookshop, as the Penguin Paperback, run by Iain Murray. All
three of them were just near the university. Evidently,
Smith's had bought Stenhouse to keep out rivals. Jack's
idea was if he ran it under a different name then the
academics would think there was good competition. If they
fell out with one, they'd go up to the other. And it actually
worked. Academics are sometimes a bit stupid. All three
of these shops were just near the university. The largest,
a little down the road in Gibson Street, was given a new
shop front and called the Arts Faculty Bookshop, whilst
the third, still with its long-serving staff who knew many
of the older academics, became the Medical Bookshop.
As Jack Knox hadn't really been interested in academic
bookselling, he left me to do as I wished, which was a

blessing. A problem arose in that each department within the company never received any financial information on their monthly stock and sales figures. One day he rang me up to say, 'Do you know that your purchases at cost exceed your total sales to date by £28,000?' Well, I didn't. But the lesson was learnt for the future.

TAKING CHARGE

I moved down to St Vincent Street, and Jack Knox said: 'I'm going to retire in a month's time, so you'd better learn the business', and I thought, 'Well, that's a bit strange, because I think I know the business pretty well.' I thought that I would always have him lingering in the background, as he was proposing to remain as chairman. I must say, to give him his due, he did come back and chair the board, but despite my doing all the things that he had steadfastly refused to do over the previous decade, he never inquired into detail and never ever criticised what was proposed. It must have sent him round the bend, but changes obviously had to be undertaken. Most of the senior staff were with me, and the younger ones too, particularly the junior managers. After I had been managing director for about seven years, Jack Knox said to me one board meeting, 'I think that you really do understand the business.' It was really kind of him, as I must have caused him much angst.

We changed a lot of things: we changed the accounting system, the order systems, the layouts of the shops, the fixtures, and we started to title the shelves. One thing that Jack Knox would not do was to title the bays by subject. He firmly believed that customers would find books they never had heard of when searching for the book they wanted. Actually, they got frustrated in looking for a specific title because they didn't know where to start

looking for a specific book they wanted. Having titled all
the bays, one day the sales director of Weidenfeld and
Nicolson, David Roy, a great talker and a great bon viveur,
came into the shop. 'Oh,' he said to me, 'I see Jack's done
what I've been telling him to do for years. He's actually
labelled the bays!' I didn't say anything, apart from 'yes'.

In those days, staff would undertake whatever they
were asked to do. They didn't stop to question, and had
little or no input into what you were doing. A lot of the
staff had been there all their lives, and it turned out that
many of them had been members of the Boys' Brigade,
particularly the 76th brigade, of which Jack Knox had
been captain. If he'd seen lads who obviously had potential,
he was able to offer them a job, particularly at a time when
unemployment was high. The result was that the firm had
an incredible quality in the senior management, most of
whom had only worked for one firm and had grown up
with John Smith's. They had an integrity and a loyalty that
was unquestioned, but they weren't visionaries.

Later, things changed and decision making became
better, with fuller consultation and by taking on board
the views of the younger managers. Just before I retired,
Jack House and Anthony Kamm were writing a history of
the firm. To do so, they, and Anthony in particular,
interviewed many long-serving members of staff. One of
the managers, Jimmy Hogg, told him: 'When Mr Clow
came, there was considerable resentment that he came in
at the top, and when he imposed the new order system I
thought it wasn't going to work, but after three months I
changed my mind.' But having been put in at the top, it
was only a nominal position, as I had no authority, and
my salary reflected this. That remained the position until
Jack Knox retired.

THE BOARD

On being invited to join the board, I found there were another two members – unpaid initially, but after a year or two, fees of £50 were agreed, which I found very welcome on top of my £10 weekly salary. The others were long-standing friends of Jack Knox, and informal board meetings were usually held to note a past event or decision that had already been taken. The board didn't really function as a board. Meetings were held in a very informal and jocular atmosphere, just really meetings to consider such items as the draft annual accounts. They were held in Wendy's, a slightly embarrassing Glasgow chain of teahouses frequented by genteel ladies and, from the odd bowler hat or two on the coat stands, a few accountants and businessmen. It turned out, evidently, that at one of these informal board meetings one of the directors had said to Jack Knox: 'You'd better look for a successor, because one day you are going to die.' This was the man who I thought was the least sharp of the three, but it proved later not to be so. He was a family lawyer who turned out to be the most perceptive of the directors and was a staunch friend to me. In addition, if it hadn't been for him, I would never have been offered a job in John Smith's and had all the interest that has added to my life.

There was always a great rush to get the annual accounts out on time. The bookkeeping and accounting practices were so complicated, what with all these thousands of credit accounts and a supply source of more than 10,000 publishers, that the senior auditor's clerkess, Miss Bendall, worked permanently throughout the year, auditing Smith's accounts for the previous year. There was also always a rush to hold the annual general meeting before the expiry of the twelve-month period after the previous year's end.

Fortunately, few, if any, shareholders turned up for the event, much to our relief. Later, greater sophistication was sought for the location of board meetings, and these were held after or during a very late lunch, in the Ceylon Tea Centre in Buchanan Street, where you got good and generous helpings of fresh salads.

Having been appointed to the board and eventually following Jack Knox, the continuity of a family firm – which had been in existence since 1751, owned by only two families and run by six managing directors (or the eighteenth-century equivalent) drawn from those families – was broken, as I was an employee. However, I do believe that companies should be owned largely by those who work in them, whenever practicable. I saw no reason why staff shouldn't become shareholders. So we went down that avenue, very cautiously in retrospect, of inviting those who'd been in the company for twenty years or more to become shareholders. Later on, that was extended, and everyone who had been with the company for five years was invited to become a shareholder. As the company increased in size and profitability, bonus shares were issued. But in the early days we asked staff to pay for their shares, and I think, in retrospect, that it might have been more generous to give them shares. However, I had to build up my own holding out of my salary of £15 a week, before tax, my then salary as assistant managing director.

St Vincent Street

Since 1751 the location of John Smith's, starting in King Street, had moved to different areas in Glasgow's city centre, usually following the centre of commerce as it moved northwards and westwards. The premises at 57 St Vincent Street had been purchased by Jack Knox's father in 1924. He paid something like £40,000 for them, which in those days was an awful lot of money. He had gone to his friends and invited them to subscribe shares, in addition to borrowing money from the bank, so the company had a fair number of somewhat wealthy but second- or third-generation shareholders, who were content for a good bookshop to be managed, rather than being concerned with obtaining a generous dividend. The company was very lucky, because it owned the freehold, and by the time I came on the scene it had paid off the bank loan. But due to the poor return on bookselling, the decor of the shop hadn't been addressed since 1924 and, I suspect, the bookshelves and cases were those inherited from the previous shops at the time of acquisition. One side had reputedly been a ladies' discreet lingerie shop, and it had glass cases in which stationery, expensive pens and fancy stationery items were displayed. These and the bookcases on the west side of the shop were twelve feet high, in a cavernous space that had sixteen-feet high ceilings. Bookshelf space was at a premium, and books were stocked and sold from these heights, a somewhat impracticable situation. Paperbacks were kept by series, rather than by author – more convenient for stocktaking and preferred by publishers. Our Penguin paperbacks, in alphabetical order, started with 'A' at twelve feet off the floor. Sales of the authors whose names ran from A to G were naturally rather limited, as access was impossible. Alison Baxter was our Penguin girl in those days, and I remember poor Alison juggling with one display copy to the front, spine on, and several stock copies behind. One day she badly snagged her nylons (then still fairly expensive) on the rickety old timber ladders, about ten feet tall, which had probably been there in 1924, too! I debated over offering to refund the cost of a new pair but had a premonition that Jack Knox would refuse, so the offer was never made. Really, you know, Health and Safety would have gone mad if they'd been in existence in those days.

When Jack Knox retired, the first thing we did was to refit the bookshop with more modern shelving (Remploy's quality bookshelves) and to bring the upper height down to eight feet. The west half of the shop had reputedly been a coach-paint shop at some time in its history. Blow me down, when we removed the high shelves we found a fireplace and mantelpiece behind them, filthy with dust, and on the latter were a coach painter's calling cards, beautifully embossed. We refitted the shop. Later, in the early 1980s, we put in new mezzanine floors to get the benefit of the high ceilings. These alterations proved to be an absolute nightmare, as we had to 'Box and Cox' departments, shuttering off half the shop with so-called dustproof screens, which left demolition dust oozing through every sheet of hardboard's joints. I remember coming into work every day and finding about half an inch of dust from the previous day's demolitions. It was absolutely awful. The staff tried to clean each morning, but the builders appeared incapable of sealing joints in hardboard to floors and ceilings. Halfway through the morning, another ceiling might come down in the half of the building where the workmen were struggling to work, and the selling area would be thick with a fog-like dust for half an hour. How staff stood it, let alone customers, I really do not know. It was absolutely awful. Fortunately, customers had little choice about where else to go to, as the Grant Educational bookshop specialised in school books and had a very poor selection of general books, which was the field in which we specialised.

It did, however, remind me of the earlier days in John Smith's. In the 1960s, Glasgow was so filthy. I remember going to work in a white shirt, with stiff cutaway starched collars – very smart, I thought. These were supplied from a highly specialised shop around the corner, called Collars Limited, but by twelve o'clock your cuffs were filthy and collars almost equally dirty. If you were going out in the evening, you had to change your clothes again at six o'clock, so you were looking fairly clean, at least on the collar, if not at the cuffs. All the book stock had to be wrapped in thin blue paper to keep it clean, and that just grew dust on the top packet. Of course, when you touched the packets or took the blue paper off, the first thing you did was to dirty your cuffs, then dirty the books that had been within the wrapping paper the moment they were touched or unwrapped.

We had a stock room down in the basement, run by an entirely Catholic staff of young lads with a Protestant manager: that's another thing I will come to in a moment, if I may. If the book wasn't on the shelf upstairs, you had to run down to the stock room, then return to the shop level. If unsuccessful, you had to pore through all the annual catalogues and latest issues of the *Bookseller* to see if you could find the bibliographical details and then be able to order the book in question. Meantime, your hands were filthy and the catalogue got filthy. It really was pretty awful. What the pollution did to the lungs was anyone's guess. Next to the stock room was the section where the delivery boys worked. One of these, before my time, was Billy Connolly. He lasted for a fortnight. It must have been one of his first jobs, and he mentions it in his autobiography. However, neither he nor older members of the company can remember why he was sacked. I suspect it was for

being cheeky to the manager, a rather strong-willed Mr
MacMillan!

I remember asking Jack Knox why it was that all the packing and stock staff were Catholic. He said, 'Oh, the two
wouldn't mix', so all the bookselling staff were Protestants
and the basement staff Catholics. In the early days, the
managing director undertook all the interviews for new
staff, in addition to the personnel work. Jack Knox used
to put on the application form 'Place of Worship' or
'Religion'. He really went into some detail about people's
personal beliefs. I suppose Jack thought that if they'd
been brought up well then they would be more likely to
be honest, but I don't know if that ran through the back
of his mind. He didn't mind if they were Catholic or
Protestant. He just said that the two wouldn't work
together, as part of the 'terrace syndrome' in football,
translated to the bookshop. One of the first things I did
was stop asking people their religion, but of course the
moment that you ask what school they went to in Glasgow,
you know whether they are Catholic or Protestant. That
issue fortunately had died by the 1970s. I remember in
the early days when I was doing the interviews for staff –
the managing director did all the personnel work and all
the salary increases and what have you – and I remember
this very nice lady who was going to join us. I explained
how one had to work in those days a five-and-a-half-day
week, and one had to come in on Saturday, and she said
to me: 'I can't come in on a Saturday,' and I said 'Why
not?' and she said: 'Don't you know?' And I said: 'What?'
and she said: 'I'm Jewish', and I said: 'No?' 'Can't you tell
by my name?' she said, and I said 'No!' and I really felt
very green. I said she could work the five days and not
the Saturday. The next thing was to establish an annual

salary review, to stop the incessant flow of 100 members of staff, one by one, asking for a rise, which had so immobilised Jack's time.

Bookshop Departments

After Mr Saville moved to the university shop, Jack Knox decided to invite one of the new-book staff, Ann Stewart, to run his former department, in which we sold all the general and art books. She was a wonderful woman who had been one of the few ladies in her year at Glasgow University in the 1920s. She was a High Anglican, so the religious section reflected her interest. Anything that theologically was directed to High Episcopalianism was in stock. Of course her favourite customer was Sister Marianne de Vane, who was a devout nun from [Roman Catholic] Notre Dame College. She was always complaining that we had quite the wrong books in stock! But she did it so courteously. I am sure she prayed daily for Miss Stewart's conversion, as that would have given her access to a different selection of books on religion, but it wasn't successful.

The manager of the department was responsible for everything that went on in his or her department. This included the buying, and obviously if one had an enthusiasm for a particular author or subject, this interest was reflected in the quality of the stock and the number of an author's titles stocked, as one liked to talk to customers about the authors who caught one's enthusiasm. I'm sure every book manager did that. My only regret was that I was never asked to run the new-book department. I would have loved to have undertaken it, but it wasn't to be. The trouble was that being shunted up to the university bookshops when Mr Saville died gave me six years' experience of academic bookselling.

However, it did prove to be invaluable in the longer run, because the academic world started to expand rapidly in line with government policy on higher education. I had the experience and was able to discuss the problems and possible solutions to academic bookselling not only with the university librarians but also with principals and vice principals. This took the company more seriously into academic bookselling, and the firm expanded into running the Glasgow University bookshop and on to Stirling University, St Andrews, Dundee, Strathclyde, Glasgow Caledonian University, Paisley and also down to Ayr, at Craigie College. The result was that turnover rose considerably and rapidly – the only limitation being the training and supply of new managers and staff. One or two brought in from bookshops down south proved to be unsatisfactory.

THE ANTIQUARIAN SECTION

When I first joined John Smith, the antiquarian section was in the basement of the house opposite (John Smith's town house), on the other side of St Vincent Street. The technical department was above, on the ground floor. Both shops, I recall, were fitted out with secondhand pine timber, not exactly quality shop fittings. There was an excellent manager in the form of Bill Strachan, who had been with the firm since he was a youngster when he had trained as an antiquarian bookseller under his predecessor, George Matthew. I never met the latter, but I understand he was an excellent bookseller, as was Bill Strachan. He was in the unique position of having access to as much of the shop's working capital as he needed. He had no budget and worked in an extraordinarily trusted manner, as would an owner of an antiquarian bookshop. But he knew his market. He knew what he could get for a book in Glasgow and knew what he could sell both to the public and to the trade that came up from the south. He also ran an out-of-print search service. When we refitted the whole shop, the department moved back into 57 St Vincent Street, initially in the basement, then on the third floor, finally ending up on the top floor. Cooper Hay, now of Cooper Hay Books in Bath Street, was the lad who followed Bill Strachan when the latter retired. On his application form, when joining the firm, he was asked what he wished to do with his life. His written reply was: 'The pursuit of knowledge'! He picked up the antiquarian trade very quickly, and eventually started up his own business with the good wishes of the company. In turn, he was followed by George Newlands, who after three years, set up his own business in Helensburgh. Ross McKenzie was our last manager. By this time we had devised a system of recording that gave us a tight control of the finances in that dangerous situation where the manager had unlimited use of capital. Mr McKenzie resigned.

We never knew in the earlier days if we made a profit with antiquarian books, because one thing we didn't do was to undertake cost accounting for the various departments. When we finally got round to it we got quite a nasty shock, because we found we didn't! Worse still, we found we were actually losing money in one of the firm's subsidiaries, Wylie's bookshop on Sauchiehall Street, run by one of the directors, Ross Higgins. He was a man of great charm, a bon viveur and an excellent raconteur of stories, but he could also be very rude if he wished so to be! He was very much his own man and told customers what they should be reading. If you liked a strong personality to sell you books, then that was grand. As Jack Knox once put it remarkably bluntly to me: 'There are refugees who come to John Smith's from Wylie's, because they can't abide him.' However, he was a very good bookseller, and if he liked a book such as Gavin Maxwell's *Ring of Bright Water*, he could sell a huge number of copies, and he landed a separate order for 450 copies of that title for one customer to give at Christmas. He really ran his own fiefdom, and Jack Knox just let him get on with it. Wylie's was a separate company and it published its own accounts, but then John Smith's did all its accounting and all its bill paying, National Insurance and wages, so those sort of things weren't charged out in the earlier days. When the rent went up from £850 per annum, the level for the previous twenty-five years, to £18,000, we could not afford to continue to run the business, and it was moved and absorbed into John Smith's.

MEETING AUTHORS

After Jack Knox had retired, we started organising auto-graph sessions. Authors and publishers' sales directors were all in favour and liked the publicity. The events could be a wonderful success or an unmitigated disaster. However, it was a great pleasure to come across all sorts of extraordinary people, like Ian Fleming, in earlier days, and later those such as Lauren Bacall, Laurens van der Post, Bernard Levin, Margot Fontaine and Edward Heath. The Heath event was perhaps our most successful, Margot Fontaine's the most pleasurable, launched on a few bottles of champagne accompanied with great charm and kind-ness. We arranged for Mr Heath to come to Glasgow for a signing session for his book on sailing. Willie Anderson, who then ran the general books department, had worked hard on promoting the session, when his mother suggested that some of her local ladies in the Borders Conservative

Association were thinking of coming to the signing. That, you know, triggered off a suggestion that there might also be a political interest in the book, so we wrote to all the Tory Associations to advertise that he would be in Glasgow. The result was that we sold 1,500 copies in pre-taken orders, and at the signing session sold at least half of these to the public on the day. The queue stretched down two sides of our block. We would have sold more, but the wretched publisher thought we had over-ordered and sent our supplementary order for a further 500 copies to another bookseller. The result was that Heath had to go up and down the queue, still snaking out of the front door and round into Mitchell Street, saying, 'I'm terribly sorry, chaps, you know, we're having to get more copies up from London. Just leave your name and address and I'll sign them before they come up and, you know, you'll get your copies.' However, we missed selling a few hundred more, which was extremely annoying.

We took him to lunch at the Malmaison, Glasgow's best restaurant, at 3 p.m. Fortunately, we had pre-ordered the meal, and because it was Heath and Glasgow, they had kept open the large dining room. It was completely empty, apart from one table. It was a Thursday afternoon, and when we came out of the restaurant it was rather late, about 5 p.m. We knew he was due at Menzies in Edinburgh for another session at that time, but there was nothing we could do. We were greeted by two building workers slightly the worse for wear. In those days, for some reason or other, builders were paid on a Thursday. As they lolled down Hope Street towards us, one said, 'There's Ted. Good old Ted.' The other said, 'Welcome to Glasgow.' Heath turned to me and said, 'There you are. It's what I've always said. They like me in Glasgow, not like those frosty buggers in

Edinburgh.' We'd had a press conference before we'd had the signing session, and he'd spent three quarters of an hour talking to some boring journalist from some third-rate, unheard-of Paisley paper. Heath was a decent man. We left him on the steps of John Smith's as he drove off in a maroon Rolls, heading for Edinburgh. I don't know at what time he arrived at Menzies. It was the beginning of the rush hour, and there were still about 200 people on the pavements opposite our bookshop. And I don't know what happened to those who must have had to wait for more than an hour in another queue, waiting for the maroon Rolls Royce to arrive at Menzies' door.

OTHER BOOKSELLERS

Our main competitor was Grant Educational in Union Street, but it specialised, so our bookshops and it really complemented each other. In Glasgow, other competition came partly from Porteous, after Jacksons Bookshop was subsumed into W. & R. Holmes. Porteous specialised in maps, magazines and sailing books, but it was a very small shop at the entrance to Royal Exchange Square. Our principal competition came from outside Glasgow – the Economist Bookshop in London, Blackwell's and Heffers – particularly when the emphasis of the firm moved towards academic bookselling. We never considered Thin's in Edinburgh to be our competitors, but after expanding in several universities throughout the central belt, I remember we once tried to buy the Edinburgh Bookshop when it came on the market. I said to the vendors, 'Have you checked with the local booksellers?' They said they had, but none of them were interested. So we negotiated, sorted out the finance, but unfortunately Willie Anderson and I were seen in Edinburgh by an ex-member of our staff, who then apparently spread the news. The first thing we knew was from our manager in St Andrews, who phoned up that same afternoon to tell us that rumour had it we were about to buy the Edinburgh Bookshop. The next day, or a few days later, we were about to sign the final agreement, when the vendors came on the phone to say they weren't gazumping us but we would have to offer more, as they had received a larger late offer. Five minutes later, Ainslie Thin came on the phone to dissuade us from the purchase: 'I hear you are going to buy the Edinburgh Bookshop.' We said: 'We've been told that nobody is interested in Edinburgh.' He said: 'I'd rather you didn't,' and we said, 'Well, Ainslie, twenty years ago one could have said, well, okay, right, but now the situation is different and our board has decided to go ahead.' And he said: 'Well, we'll open in Glasgow,' and I said, 'Do what you want to. I don't mind'. But we did our sums again and came to the conclusion that the new price we would have to beat was too great if we were ever going to make any money, so we pulled out and Thin's acquired the shop, only to be hit by the opening of the huge Waterstone's at the other end of George Street and a large W. H. Smith's shortly afterwards. So we were very glad that the rumour had spread so rapidly, though at the time we found the thought of opening in Edinburgh to be rather stimulating! I am just very sorry that we unnecessarily must have caused Ainslie Thin a sleepless night or two; that's the last thing I'd ever want to do, because I am very fond of him.

We exchanged trade information, statistics and financial information with Heffers bookshop in Cambridge. It was a family firm, as was Thin's, which made their philosophy different from ours, but Thin's was probably too close for that sort of exchange. The retired managing director of

Heffers told me very recently that they looked on us as one of their competitors, in spite of the exchange of information, which I suppose was a sort of compliment. But when we discussed overseas activities they would clam up. The book trade was getting more and more efficient, and in due course we closed our antiquarian section because it didn't pay, only to find that Heffers had taken the same step. By that time we were coming under economic pressures, and business was getting smarter and competition keener. When I first went into the book trade, I thought that the publishing side was fairly well organised and the book trade disorganised. After twenty-five years in the trade, I felt that the roles had been reversed: publishers were less efficient than the leading booksellers, and it was fairly clear that power in the trade was moving towards the retail side, rather than the production side; that is to say, out of the hands of publishers, if the bookseller was sufficiently large.

New Blood

By this time, the 1980s and early 1990s, we'd got really good young managers coming up, people like Martin Waters, his wife Fiona, Willie Anderson, John Farrow and Stuart Johnston, to mention a few. The only trouble was that any time there was a marital break-up one of the pair inevitable went off and worked in Heffers! The company was getting much better organised, and financially we were much more under control. As time went on, the financial control got even better and better, as we had a brilliant accountant, Peter Notarangelo, towards the end. Martin Waters applied his librarian's well-ordered mind to our systems and the manner in which he organised his department, general books. Willie Anderson ran the paperback department, which had been considerably expanded. When Martin Waters left us, Willie took over the new-book department. He generated a great loyalty from the staff, great enthusiasm for books, and he was a very good talker. In due course he was appointed to the board, along with Ross Higgins and John Gordon, and I felt we had a quality of management that was very high. We could continue to expand, provided we had the managerial personnel who understood the company's philosophy and systems, but that wasn't to be.

OLD TECHNOLOGY

When I first came into the trade, bookselling, for those not already doing it, was perceived to be a job for the gentle and the genteel and those who liked a clean job. In fact, it was filthy dirty. It was also very hard physical work, because you were carrying boxes of books round the shop and up and down stairs, most of them the size of Penguin boxes, more than full, and all throughout the day. In John Smith's main bookshop (St Vincent Street) there was a broad strip of lino, brown lino, that stretched to the back of the shop, on which customers generally walked, but if they were viewing the books on huge long, panelled and varnished Victorian stands, like oblong coffins prepared for giants in some previous epoch, they would walk on the building's original bare timber floors. There were four of these vast stands on either side of the brown lino strip, dead in line, which marched down to the end of the shop. Stacked on the floor, or on boards raised an inch or two, piles of new publications collected dust and other dirt in front of these stands or behind them. Sometimes books at the bottom of the piles were still wrapped in that blue paper. In those days a subscription order might be for as many as 500 copies of the latest Ian Fleming, or even 750. It frequently became a matter of prestige for both a publisher's rep and for the bookshop, but the problem was where to stock them. Our cleaning staff used to come in every evening and put down wet tea from some local restaurant like the Ceylon Tea Centre, which they would then brush up. The wet tea was to keep the dust down, which of course it didn't. Dust got into the books, and the damp tea, if incorrectly thrown, stained the dust jackets! Occasionally the floors would be mopped using an old-fashioned rag or string-head mop. The inevitable happened. The books became splattered with water the colour of dirty brown lino! Next morning all the piles had to be dusted again.

Working hours were fairly standard in those days. It would be 9 to 5.30, and you got an hour and a half off for lunch, sufficient time to take a tram back to the West End, have lunch at home, and return in time to relieve the next member of staff. Younger staff used to read and remain in town for the hour and a half, as we were encouraged to read what we were trying to sell, having first of all booked the book out. With the demise of the tram system, staffing arrangements became more complicated, and gradually the lunch break was shortened to an hour, then to half an hour in exchange for a five-day week, with managers trying to schedule lunch breaks to keep the shop as fully staffed as possible during the busy times.

While we were working five and a half days a week, we all got Saturday afternoon free, so complications arose when the shop opened all day on Saturdays, as the shopping patterns in the city centre changed, and Saturday, from being one of the quietest days, with light, mornings-only takings, gradually became our best day. However, some people preferred to have a day off during the week when other shops were quieter, but all the time it was change, change, change and trying to improve our service. We had this aim of endeavouring to run the best bookshop north of Oxford. (You couldn't compete with Blackwell's.) So that's what we tried to do, until we started to flirt with computerisation.

New Technology

I kept away from computers, thinking it was a younger man's toy. Willie Anderson was more involved, along with Stuart Johnston. Our first experience with them was an absolute disaster for us, the contracting company and the manufacturer. Several years later, we ended up trying to sue the manufacturer – for £200,000, I recall.

Needless to say, the firm slid into bankruptcy as other firms chased them. The legal system trundled on at its own slow pace, and the opposition's lawyers played for time. On every occasion (three) that we sought recourse in law we never obtained justice. Justice in the commercial world is elusive or non-existent. We had too ambitious a concept of what we wanted to do with computers, and the computers never gave us the answer we were looking for. The software contractor turned out to be a tin-pot company, although the managing director was a bookseller, which made us think he knew the trade and therefore knew what he was doing. We were wrong. We should have seen warning signs when we saw his system in Birmingham and he showed us his outstanding order file. It consisted of a quarter-full card tray. Ours was more than twenty times bigger. Things became more complex and less and less satisfactory, so we started to do some of the programming ourselves. The programmes could tell what the stock situation was, but unless the information loaded by staff was accurate, the information was wrong. I don't think staff realised at that stage just how important accuracy was. The combination of computer, paperwork and a stock exchange to supply orders rapidly between shops – by this time we had nine or ten shops throughout the central belt – led to a very complex system. The computer system became too complicated and too expensive and was nearly our undoing.

DECLINE AND FALL

After a long run of good fortune and a steady expansion of the business to more than five times its real size in volume terms, we had our first knock at the hands of Robert Maxwell, and I lost the first night's sleep of my life. We had watched his expansion carefully and had successfully outmanoeuvred him at Stirling University, where we were given the contract to run the university bookshop. We were also planning to open a bookshop at Strathclyde University, which we reckoned would take about twenty years to pay, given the magnitude of the rental, when Maxwell, under the name of his privately owned company, announced he was opening a shop about twice the size of ours, including the two units we proposed to take! At that time we didn't know he was discounting all the Pergamon Press invoices in favour of Robert Maxwell Bookshops! So it didn't matter if he lost money on the venture, as vast capital sums were flowing into his personally owned shops. When his empire collapsed, we were invited by the university to run the bookshop but in a much better location, as the university had expanded considerably under its new principal, Sir Graham Hills.

Little did we know that the Net Book Agreement would

be abandoned by the publishers, just before I retired, although we had consistently told Sir Gordon Borrie (of the so-called Office of Fair Trading) and his cohorts what would happen to the booktrade if RPM [Retail Price Maintenance] were to be abolished by the government. Publishers spared him the effort and delivered the *coup de grace.* I knew a lot of publishers were against retail price maintenance, particularly the younger ones, and so were many journalists, such as Simon Jenkins. Willie Anderson and I wrote an article for the London *Times* that it published, and several letters too, and to the *Guardian.* But if you do want good bookshops to flourish, and smaller bookshops too, plus the diversity of any particular trade, then some form of price maintenance is required in a trade where there are so many manufacturers (we had 16,000 publishers on our database) and you offer to get any book that is in print in the UK, Europe, USA and the Far East. Larger firms could push publishers for wider terms and then afford better locations and to discount, as their margins became wider and wider.

We weren't to know the American predator, Borders, planned to open in Glasgow. We thought the competition would come from Dillons, but their MD undertook accounting practices that certainly we wouldn't take and was dismissed rather rapidly by his chairman. In the end, we had those two in addition to Waterstone's under Tim Waterstone. In the meantime, we had opened our some-what trendy bookstore, Volumes, in Queen Street, so Glasgow was suddenly awash with new bookshops. We thought we could see off Dillons and Waterstone's, but Borders had a vast stock of the magnitude that we could never have afforded and for which I did not believe there was a market in Glasgow. However, they chose the best site in Glasgow – and also the most expensive to date – and opened up, having secured trade terms better than those we were being given. They just vacuumed customers out of St Vincent Street, which looked old-fashioned and cramped, and they also had an effect on our sales as far away as Byres Road, in the West End. Sales kept dropping, and the company bled millions over three years, rapidly eroding our capital base that had been carefully built up over the past thirty years.

The bank became agitated and pushed us to realise the value of our two properties to pay off the overdraft, so the decision was taken to sell the academic part of the business to Blackwell's and the export side to one of the exporting companies down south. Blackwell's had recently bought out Heffers, reputedly for £10 million, and were apparently having problems digesting it. They were only interested in the Glasgow University bookshop, and possibly the Strathclyde one. Strangely, they told me, they were interested in Thin's. However, they couldn't make up their minds and dithered and swithered, as there were internal family fiscal difficulties at the time. The problem was solved by Willie Anderson and some of the senior staff coming back to the board with an offer for a staff buyout. I thought it better that the management remained in Glasgow, so it went through. But then the new company lost another huge sum of money and the business was sold to a Canadian firm. It did mean that there was a capital injection, and half the company still survived. But the Canadian company moved the export side down south and continued with just the academic side up here.

I suppose, rather stupidly, with the firm having been around for almost 250 years, we thought it would go on forever and we would be celebrating a quarter of a

millennium of independence in 2001, but it was not to
be. I remember making my will and leaving money for a
managing director or chairman's dinner after I died. One
always hoped that the next month things would turn out
better, but of course they didn't. It really was sad. And
the real tragedy was that we had fifty or sixty nice people,
real booksellers, well-trained, who knew their stock, who
all lost their stock. If I go into Borders and a title is not
on their computer, they appear to report it out of print.
That included my own book, which was listed in British
Books in Print. I asked what the database was and the girl
said: 'Oh, it's an American database!' The implications in
that dismay me.

Willie Anderson

CHANGING PROFESSIONS

I joined John Smith's in 1973, when I was twenty-five. I was married two weeks earlier, and for six years previously I had been working in the Royal Bank of Scotland in London. I suppose I really wasn't a banker – a lot of people would probably say that I am not a bookseller either – but I wasn't a banker, looking after other people's money, when I couldn't even look after my own, and it was actually a very boring life. Next door to us, in Victoria Street in London, was a little bookseller called Berger and Timms. I used to give them change, which used to annoy the accountant excessively, because they weren't customers. I used to give them change, and as a privilege of my giving them change, they used to lend me proofs of books, because they actually saw that I read, which was a very unusual thing for someone in a bank to do. Our accountant always liked to be on the golf course at 4.30 in the summer (and also in the winter too, I think). As he lived in Colchester, to get to which you had to go to Liverpool Street, which was on the other side of London from Victoria, the bank used to close at about quarter to four in the afternoon, between half three and four. There really wasn't an awful lot to do, so I used to go round to Berger and Timms after the bank closed and help tidy up shelves and help out, unpaid, if I wasn't playing rugby or something like that.

When I met my future wife, we decided we didn't want to live in London any more, and she suggested I tried to get into something to do with books. The classic thing was to try publishing, but as I wasn't a graduate there wasn't a hope in hell in those days of getting into publishing. I failed miserably every time I tried. So I wrote off to three booksellers in Scotland: James Thin, John Menzies – which wasn't really a bookseller – and John Smith's. John Smith's gave me an interview and gave me a job. I'm Glasgow born and bred, so I suppose that is how it all came about. But why I came into bookselling, I have no idea. I came from a family that has always read books, and I went to a school were books were very important. Literature has always been part of my life. Books have always been a fascinating part of my life.

ENTERING JOHN SMITH & SON

I was interviewed by a chap called Ross Higgins, who I think was more interested in what school I went to rather than what I was capable of, but he also happened to know somebody I knew, which I suppose helped. No renovations had been done in the old John Smith's on St Vincent Street, so it was a very old-fashioned looking bookshop: it had very high shelving with library steps and all other sorts of things. It had a lift in the ground floor, the ground floor side nearest to Buchanan Street, right bang in the middle. It was a very slow lift operated by a lift-man called Geoff Martin. I remember getting onto the lift to go up to the interview on the third floor, and the handle was switched, and the lift started to rise. Then there was this almighty noise from the lift and I realised that the lift-man had fallen asleep and was snoring between the ground floor and the third floor. This was my introduction to John Smith's before my interview: from the glitzy world of banking to the rather different world of bookselling.

I joined John Smith's as an assistant in what was then called the college department in the basement which was right next to Goods Inwards, so I learnt very quickly Glasgow's swearing patois. I also learnt some of the more interesting aspects of Glasgow education. I think the first question I was ever asked was in the college department. We basically served further education students rather than university students, but the first question I was asked was: did I have this book by Shakespeare called *MacBeth Cider with Rosie Laurie Lee*? I tried to point out to the student that this was in fact two books and was told very firmly that I didn't know what I was talking about.

THE WORKING DAY

I was basically on the shop floor. Yes, I joined as a shop assistant in 1973, nothing grand, no plans, nothing, I didn't know how long I was going to last there. I remember taking a massive drop in salary to join John Smith's. It was quite a different way of life: you didn't have Carnaby Street and you didn't have shops. I came from a world where banking had retreated into a nine to four o'clock routine, depending on which branch you were in London, with no Saturday work. I entered a job where you started at nine o'clock, when the shop opened, until five thirty, and even at that time John Smith's had just started to open all day Saturday. So we worked a Saturday off, then a half Saturday, and then a full Saturday. If you did a full Saturday, you got a day off in the previous week; basically you worked a ten-and-a-half-day fortnight. Those were basically your hours, so it didn't do much for my rugby career, and so I didn't play very much.

It was very physical, extremely physical job. People always say when they go into bookselling that they like books and they envisage themselves sitting in a corner reading all the books that they can possibly find in life. That is perfectly possible to do if that's what you want to do, but books are actually extraordinarily heavy items. If you actually think about a bookshop, it has probably the most heavy industrial loading that you can possibly have if you have floors. The job was an extraordinarily physical thing: books came in boxes, publishers used to deliver these boxes to you, and you just had to hump them around the bookshop. You built up these muscles that you didn't know you had. I remember when I first went into bookselling I was absolutely exhausted for the first four months because I hadn't done so much physical labour and walking. You also did a tremendous amount of walking, probably walking somewhere in the region of eight to ten miles a day, depending on how busy the shop was, because you are just walking backwards and forwards around the shop, picking up books for customers, putting books away, tidying shelves, doing this, going up stairs to find cash, all these sorts of things. You are actually on the move the whole time.

Basically you came in in the morning, you put your books away, you tidied, you made sure that all the stock cards were tidied, then you got round to doing a stock check, you passed orders on to the department manager or the bookshop manager to process. You didn't do anything exciting like ordering books in those days.

WILLIE ANDERSON

THE DEPARTMENTS

I graduated from the basement in about five weeks. They decided that I wasn't so dishevelled and disgusting to the general public, so they allowed me onto the ground floor, into the general book department, which was a really exciting department in John Smith's, because it had all the novels and the biographies and the cooking books. I met a fascinating group of customers. You were always being asked questions about books and whether you liked them, so it was always a much more interesting aspect. But the ground floor was ruled by ladies of a certain age who had never married. There was one lady who looked after the religious section, called Miss Russ, who lived with her elderly mother at that time. Miss Russ always refused to serve a customer at half past one, or refused to answer the telephone after half past one, because she had to leave the shop bang on two o'clock, because if she wasn't back by two thirty her mother would get her into trouble. She must have been in her sixties. So it was really quite difficult in the religious section; after one thirty there wasn't really much religion going around if a customer asked a question of Miss Russ at that particular moment in time.

There was a lady called Miss Parker who ran the cookery section, and God forbid anybody who touched the cookery section without her authority or took a book, or served a customer. There was Miss Buist, who was the cashier. She lived in a little sort of tower with a front door. It was a bit like Grace Brothers [from *Are You Being Served*, a popular television comedy of the 1980s, set in an exaggeratedly old-fashioned department store], I suppose, because the customer used to take a book and hand over a pound note for, say, a new novel at twelve and six or whatever, and she would give back the change herself. You

41

weren't allowed anywhere near the till – only this one lady to handle everything. She kept an eagle eye on everything in the shop, and she would shout down to Martin Waters, the manager of the department at the time: 'Mr Waters! I don't think Mr Anderson is working very hard at the moment, I think you could give him something else to do!' So that was really how the ground floor worked in those days; it was really quite fun.

It was an extraordinarily Victorian experience. It really was sort of like stepping back in time. I even remember my first day in the Royal Bank of Scotland, too, because the first job I had in the Royal Bank of Scotland was in Trafalgar Square, and this was in 1967, and I remember going in there and all the tellers wore Eton collars, and there was snuff on the counter. Basically, London had moved on a wee bit. I came up to John Smith's, and it really was another step back in time. There was no evidence that it had really changed since the pre-war days, but things did then develop after that.

THE MANAGEMENT

I only met Jack Knox twice in my life. Once when I tried to throw what I thought was a tramp out of the shop at about twenty-five to six, only to discover that he was the chairman of the company – which didn't go down particularly well. I didn't have the faintest idea who he was. He wasn't particularly well dressed. His coat was a bit stained. But as soon as he spoke to me I realised I had made a terrible mistake. Anyway, I still survived. The only other time I met him was when I had taken over the paperback department and sales had shot up rather extraordinarily. He came down to say that he was very pleased to see that the sales had shot up. He was a very distant figurehead at this stage, because obviously he had retired from the company.

Robert Clow was then the managing director of the company: young, eccentric, very energetic. He could be quite a humorous man as well. He could also be extremely dogmatic. He had ideas that were probably ahead of their time as far as bookselling was concerned. He had ambition for John Smith's and its position in Glasgow society. You have to remember that bookselling in those days was completely different from bookselling now. You basically had a major independent family type of bookseller in most of the major towns in Britain. Edinburgh had Thin's, Aberdeen had Bissetts, Dundee had Russell's at that particular moment in time – if you think of Heffers in Cambridge, Austicks in Leeds, Georges in Bristol. John Smith's was Glasgow's equivalent of that. There was Grant's as well in Union Street. But Robert had a vision of bookselling, and of the quality of bookselling, that could be brought to Glasgow. Basically that required a very different shop from what we had. It required a complete refit.

You can imagine that, when I first joined John Smith's in 1973, there were five floors in the building, a very huge gap between the ground floor and the first floor, and huge ceilings, because basically the building was a conversion of old shops and offices. The first floor at that particular time was the academic department, basically serving Strathclyde University, and the basement was the technical department, also serving Strathclyde. It was when we started to do the renovations in 1975 and 1976 that it was realised that the first floor with all the academic books on it was actually very heavily bowed, with the weight of the books, and the joints were only just resting on the most infinitesimal amount of space. There was every likelihood that the floor could have collapsed at any moment in time. You actually could see it bowing at certain times of the year, especially when you had lots of books in place, because it was never constructed to be a bookshop, and of course the weight of books was groaning, groaning, groaning. It was quite necessary, therefore, that the shop was renovated. This was a huge undertaking by Robert and the board at that point in time, and I also suspect the staff were expected to endure quite a lot whilst this under-taking was going on. The canteen was on what was then the fifth floor and then became the sixth floor, because we put in an extra floor, but you had to walk across a plank from what was the new fire exit across to what was the canteen. Of course, Health and Safety in those days was not quite what it is nowadays. It really was like being pirates at sea walking across this rather feeble plank to get to the canteen.

THE PAPERBACK DEPARTMENT

The paperback department was a strange entity when I first went into John Smith's. It was actually a paperback department, but there seemed to be more volumes of poetry than anything else because the manager liked poetry. Paperbacks were not in those days considered to be books. You'd get customers coming in 1973 or 1974 saying: 'I don't want the paperback, I want the book, please.' The paperback department was not really a very strong part of John Smith's. The manager at that particular time decided to leave. I was offered the job and a pay rise of about £100 a year, or something. So I took it on. The first representative I had to see was a guy called Alec Bilsland, who was the Pan representative at the time. Alec came in and said, 'Right, where's the subscriptions?' and so I started going through it, and by the time he'd finished he said: 'Do you realise that in this one subscription you have ordered more than John Smith's has done in the past two years of orders?' But it was great, because it was a very easy job.

I was in charge of the paperback department, and you couldn't fail to succeed in it, because the previous figures had been so rotten. It just came down basically to ordering. It was also a great time, as paperbacks were taking off in people's consciousness. New books like *Zen and the Art of Motorcycle Maintenance* were coming through. I remember taking 200 copies of that and Robert just about sacking me for it, but it was 200 copies more than anyone else took in Scotland, I think. We sold out within ten days, which saved my life. But it was also at this time that Penguins were published on the last Thursday of every month. It was a huge event, because any book that was worth reading was then published by Penguin. Pan started to come through; and it was an exciting time. You had Penguin Classics, Pelicans, the Penguins themselves. As long as you kept to a routine of ordering and were aware of what was going on and generally tried to make life a bit more interesting for the public, the paperbacks were there to be sold. We increased sales in the first year by something like 60 per cent – it wasn't particularly hard.

We were also, at that time, the first bookseller to get involved in Melvyn Bragg's programme *Read All about It*. I have kept a friendship with Melvyn since those days, and with Nigel Williams, who was the researcher on the programme. It was the first television programme that really captured the public's imagination about books. It was, when I look back at it now, an elitist programme, but it kept people's enthusiasm going. I remember the time

45

when Antonia Fraser reviewed Isaac Bashevis Singer's *The Slave* that was in Penguin. The queue outside the shop in the morning, waiting for that book on the Monday after the programme appeared, was quite extraordinary. We'd ordered thirty copies of it, and I think the Penguin rep thought I was mad to even order thirty. Of course, in those days Bashevis Singer was a cult author, but that book went on to sell vast quantities because of the programme. I was always conscious of the fact that publishers get a lot of publicity, authors get a lot of publicity, but the booksellers that actually sold the book never seemed to get any recognition for it all. So I wrote off to *Read All about It* and saying, 'How about mentioning the bookshops because actually we do a lot of the selling. There weren't any other places that sold books apart from booksellers, so how about giving us credit too?' We actually got on, and after that they always had a bookshop featured on the programme.

The paperback department was great fun, but you can only do it for a number of years before getting entirely bored, because the routine was the same. I did just over two years among the paperbacks and then I went on to the general department.

THE GENERAL DEPARTMENT

I seemed to succeed the break-up of marriages, as happened as well with the general book department. A marriage broke up, and I seemed to fall into the position the person held in the company. I took on the general book department on the same day that my first daughter was born in 1976. The department had moved from the ground floor to the basement because of the renovations that were going on. It made life slightly difficult. I had six tremendous years running that department; it was just fascinating, as it was just such an exciting part of the shop. You could get colleagues involved, and you could really start to influence the customers. Robert really supported me a tremendous amount during those years, partly because he saw I was trying to do something that was a bit more than other people were trying to do. It was almost a golden period of British publishing. You had fascinating writers like Patrick White, Salman Rushdie coming through, the likes of John Irving and John Fowles – the latter wasn't particularly popular, but he was producing novels like *Daniel Martin*. There was the growth of the cookery market, the growth of the sports market; some tremendous biographies were coming through, and it was the start of hypes, such as the *Country Diary of an Edwardian Lady*: all in all, the range of books and the quality of books were getting better and better. We still had tremendous contacts with publishing houses, such as Jonathan Cape and Chatto and Windus, and you'd get to know people like Nora Smallwood, Tom Maschler and Ion Trewin. You got to know the editors like Liz Calder. You were going through about thirteen, four-teen books a week at that time, and some of them you read from cover to cover, and some you just skimmed, but you actually knew what your books were. If you got a particularly good book from the reps, well, you just wrote off to the publisher and said how much you liked it, and what could you do about it. That got you known, and it was all part of a drive, probably a sub-conscious drive, to make John Smith's into a name in the bookselling world. I think it succeeded in doing that, because we were recognised in the general book department as prob-ably being the best place outside of Hatchards in London as a place where fiction could be sold, where Scottish books were sold, where all sorts of books were sold.

We were the first bookshop to launch author evenings in 1979, when the first author we invited was John Fowles. That was the first time he'd ever done any session in a bookshop. We cleared out the ground floor and put seats in it. We had 250 people sitting there. We followed up with Laurens van der Post a week later. Then William Trevor and others – it just followed on for years after that. I'd just gone to Robert with idea for this and said: 'I've got these people lined up, what do you think?' Robert said: 'On your head be it.' But he was very supportive, and I think you can't do these things without the support of your superiors. Robert generally was a person who always wanted to go outside of what was the norm. He looked beyond the black-and-white box towards the good things that were beyond that. If you were willing to take those chances for him, then you got his support. If you weren't prepared to take those risks, if you weren't prepared to think outside of the box, he wasn't prepared to support you. He was terrific to talk to about all these aspects and work through them with him. Quite often he himself would come up with some idea that you thought was absolutely and utterly crazy, but the annoying thing was that he was usually right. As a team you worked things through.

That is how our relationship built up, because basically we were both interested in doing things outside the box. John Smith's was the first bookshop to have a string quartet coming into the shop at lunchtime concerts on Tuesday. We even managed to get into the *Herald* as part of a promotion. We were always great believers in bookshops being part of the theatre, being part of the community, being part of what was going on. There wasn't much point in waiting for customers to come to you; you had to do things to make customers want to come to the bookshops. This was in many ways quite revolutionary, I like to think. Although that may seem boastful, not very many other people were doing anything like it round the country.

A SCOTTISH BOOKSHOP

Bill Campbell from Mainstream remains a longstanding friend. In the 1970s he worked for Polygon, or more precisely its forerunner, Edinburgh University Student Publication Board. (Gordon Brown was also on the committee.) Bill then formed his own company, Mainstream, with Peter McKenzie. The first bookseller that Bill came to was John Smith's, and the first book he'd published was Robert Louis Stevenson's *The Cévennes Journal*, a little green edition. We took one hundred copies of that, just because he was a Scottish publisher and we wanted to promote it. I remember getting very angry subsequently with Alan Massie because he'd written a letter or an article in the *Herald* which said that it was appalling how Scottish publishers were treated in Scottish bookshops – Scottish books were always on the bottom shelf. I wrote back and asked, 'Have you ever been in Glasgow's bookshops?' and he admitted no, he hadn't, that he'd been basing all this on the Edinburgh bookshops. I invited him to John Smith's, and we've been friends ever since. Bookselling was very important for Scottish publishing at that time, as it was starting to blossom: Simon Berry, Stephanie Wolfe Murray and others like Bill coming together to form the Scottish Publishers' Association.

So there was lots of interest in Scottish publishing. *Lanark* came out in 1981 from Canongate in Edinburgh. That really was a major, almost seminal, moment in Scottish publishing. Here was a home-grown author who had taken years to write this; it was a book people had known about for many years but thought would never appear. It made a huge impact upon the literary world. However, it wasn't just that sort of thing – it was amazing little books on Glasgow, on Edinburgh, wherever it was, or reminiscences of Scottish life, that actually kept Scottish booksellers going for quite a number of years. It was a very important part of our sales, especially around the Christmas period. We were able to sell an awful lot of them, and booksellers ignored those books at their peril, but some did ignore them, and that is why perhaps they are not in existence now.

BOOKSHOP MANAGER

I became manager in 1982. Robert had asked me to join the board in 1978, but no-one appointed me formally until about two years later. In the meantime, I used to attend board meetings secretly. We had to have board meetings outside the company so no-one would know that I was on the board. Robert realised there might be certain repercussions from some people, which did occur – some said that they were going to leave and they did. But there wasn't that much of a fall-out, because most people in the company recognised, fortunately, that it was not too bad a thing. With my involvement in the direction of the company, it became more and more difficult to run a floor in the way that it should be run, because attention is involved elsewhere in developments within the company and so on. So in 1982 I came off the shop floor. For a wee period I was brought back on again for about six months. I started to involve myself in more administration work and more things like the Booksellers' Association.

THE BOOKSELLERS' ASSOCIATION AND BOOKSELLERS

Bookselling in my view didn't really change until the late 1990s, after the abolition of the Net Book Agreement, because the NBA really meant that bookselling followed certain lines year in and year out. Yes, there was the growth of people like Waterstone's and Dillons, and the fluctuations of John Menzies and W. H. Smith, but there wasn't real change within the book trade. It was a very stable industry. You could basically know what the profit was going to be based on the sales. I don't think there was a lot of imagination in the trade. There were some shining examples of people who thought outside the box, and Robert was certainly one of them, but he was a fairly lone voice throughout those years. The Booksellers' Association had very much that unimaginative image, because it had to reflect booksellers; it couldn't actually influence what the trade would do, but it could act as a cohesive force for discussion, perhaps, of policy and as a lobbying force. The BA was also a good way of getting the company known around the trade, if you participated in it. You became a voice, and perhaps you could influence the trade, hopefully for the better, and try to promote books, because books are so important. Booksellers all love books; we think that books are terribly important. But for 80 or 90 per cent of the population, books are not really important. Lots of people can get by without reading books at all. So, why bother? I think the trade became extremely complacent over those years. The Booksellers' Association became complacent too, and I think that, if you wanted to change things, there was no point in shouting about it from the sidelines, you had to get inside and change things from there.

One of the great things about the book trade, whether you are a bookseller or a publisher, is that you make friends, and you make them for a long time in your life. There was always a sort of love–hate relationship between booksellers and publishers – they think that we don't read, and we think that they can't; they know nothing about business, and we know even less. We do have a commonality of product, and a commonality of interest. The publishing world was changing dramatically through the 1980s, when there were a lot of amalgamations and consolidations. Many independent publishers could no longer sustain life as it had been. There were too many books being published, too great a variety for the economics of the business; there was so much wastage in publishing, and there was so much wastage in bookselling, but the book-sellers hadn't realised at that moment in time just how much wastage there was. So the publishing industry was undergoing huge change, and I think publishers were perhaps more anxious for change within the change, but they didn't quite know how to do it. There were groups of booksellers who were also interested in change, but it was like trying to shove against a very, very thick stone wall to actually get people to move.

I think one of the most telling examples of it was the case of book tokens. We spent our lives licking the damn things to stick them onto cards, which we then had the temerity to ask the customer to pay for – this was not actually a customer-friendly thing. I don't think booksellers have taken on board the changes in customers' perceptions of what retailing was about. For many years booksellers were slow to respond to the fact that the customer is, in fact, a very important person; you need to put as few barriers to them buying the book or the product as you possibly can, rather than trying to create barriers, and stop them from buying books. Sometimes you saw some of the red tape coming through, and you thought, goodness gracious, do these people really know what it is like to be on the shop floor? One of the great things about being on the shop floor is that you must always be there to say 'yes' to the customer, and you should always be there, and it shouldn't be the person on the shop floors who has to say 'no' – they should always be able to say: 'Yes, here is the book; here is what it is; yes, I can do that for you.' And if there is ever a problem, it should be for someone more senior to deal with it; it should never be foisted downwards. Retailing is actually a very easy thing to do, if you do it properly.

THE NET BOOK AGREEMENT

I was president of the Booksellers' Association when the NBA fell, so I think that it is my lot in life to see things that have been established for a long time fall. The world had changed by 1995, and the Net Book Agreement had become unsustainable. It was, I believe, keeping the trade back. There was actually nothing you could do. You had to sell the book at that particular price: you couldn't do any promotion; you couldn't, for example, buy one book and get one free, because that was against the whole spirit of the Net Book Agreement. It really was holding the industry back compared to other areas of retail. In 1995 the bookselling trade was probably about twenty years behind the rest of the retail high street in the way that it was going. There was no opportunity for investment, no opportunity for development in the trade, and the whole trade was becoming moribund.

Publishers were becoming extraordinarily frustrated

because their markets were being limited, and they were starting to perceive things like the world wide web that were just beginning to break through. They realised at that time that their number was up. You had people outside of bookselling who wanted to sell books in a way that was widening the market. Quite rightly – booksellers don't have an exclusive right to sell books. It doesn't really matter where they are sold. If you sell the books well, you will get the customer; if you don't, you won't get the customers. There was a huge pressure on publishers in particular, because they wanted to extend their markets into other areas where booksellers were not reaching and booksellers were not going to reach. The only way that was going to happen was if books could be treated like other products on supermarket shelves.

Actually, Archie Norman was the great mover of this, as far as Asda was concerned, and Timothy Hely-Hutchison of Headline was another, but they were the figureheads, the people speaking out. There was a huge movement within the publishing industry for abolition. Publishers would tell booksellers who were listening that they wanted the Net Book Agreement to remain, when actually they wanted to get rid of it. There was an anxious moment from booksellers, who saw this as a vehicle to be able to increase their profile, increase their market share, to be able to join what else was happening on the high street. By the end, the Net Book Agreement was becoming unsustainable. It was, apart from pharmaceuticals, the only part of the business world which had retail price maintenance, and it just wasn't going to last. Having said that, publishers still set the price of books; they still print the prices on the covers of books. Paperbacks still have the price on them. The publishers still set the margins; they still exercise control.

Ainslie Thin

CAREER CHOICE

My father was a chemical analyst and I had intended to go into chemistry. I did a degree in chemistry at Edinburgh University. I was at university from 1953 to 1957. I'd really decided to join ICI. Then in my second-last year at university someone at ICI came to speak to us about careers in ICI, and this person had spent twenty-five years in unfruitful research in the chemical industry. Every soap bar, he discovered, hadn't been quite good enough to put on the market. So – and he was a miserable old fellow – I thought, I can't let myself go in for this sort of thing. At about that time my uncle spoke to my father, and said: 'Would the young man be interested in joining the business, because we need another family member?' And so I was asked about this, and I said, 'Well, I'll think about it.' I did think about it eventually. I had actually thought: if I get a first-class honours degree I'll stay in the academic world, because I don't want to join ICI. I got a second-class honours, so I joined the book business. I never told my uncle how I made the decision, but that was really how it happened. It was a decision that I never regretted.

Apprenticeship

It was arranged by my uncle that I should work with Sir Basil Blackwell at Blackwell's for six months and get some experience, which I did between September 1957 and March 1958. I worked for Blackwell's in Oxford for five months and for one month in their shop in Bristol. Then I came and joined South Bridge in March 1958. To begin with, I was given the task of preparing a mathematical catalogue for a big international mathematical conference for which we were preparing an exhibition of books. We produced a catalogue of about thirty pages or so of English, German, French, some Polish and other mathematics books – all academic books – and this was part of the offering in connection with the big exhibition of books at the conference. That kept me quiet for a while.

I remember I was put at a table in a yard downstairs that was just beside the men's loo, and every man that wanted to go to the loo had to walk past me, working away at this table. It wasn't entirely an appropriate place to work. But that was how I started out. And then gradually I just worked my way into the business.

Reforming the Business

Jimmy [James Thin, cousin to Ainslie] was almost exactly ten years older than me. He joined in 1950 and he had built up a mail-order business, mostly theological mail orders. He did that because at the end of the war American theological students came to New College, and they found that British theological books were a lot cheaper than American ones. So they went back to America after taking their degree and started buying books from us. Jimmy started producing little lists and then bigger lists, and it built up into something really quite massive, with a mailing list of about 25,000 people, mostly Presbyterian ministers in America and Canada.

It was a lot of business, a lot of work, but as we discovered later on, it was for very little profit. Initially when I joined the business, I got myself involved in the general management, and quite a lot in the mail-order business – but specifically, you could say, the scientific and technical department, which Jimmy wasn't particularly wanting to get involved in, and the stationery department, and so on. After a short time, we found that we were spending an awful lot of time on these mail orders that were flowing in. I mean, hundreds of orders, and lots of catalogues that were being produced at great cost that were being sent out to the customers all around the world. Quite often they were buying a £3 book that we didn't have in stock which had to be ordered, sent out to them, invoiced, statements had to be sent out, and at the end of the day you had to make some money out of it, but it wasn't quite so easy as that, so the turnover was increasing rapidly, and the profit was decreasing equally rapidly.

I joined the business in 1958, and by about 1964 the situation had become fairly serious. So we got the firm PA Consultancy to help us analyse the problem by breaking the business down into sections. We got the profitability of each section, and it showed dramatically that we were doing well on cash sales generally, and that the mail-order side was losing money, and also that we really needed better systems. From that point on, we concentrated much more on the cash sales; that was when we extended our children's department, brought it downstairs and made much greater effort to open up a lot of space for stocking more books.

JIMMY THIN

Once Uncle Ainslie, Jimmy's father, retired, which he did in 1962, it was really up to Jimmy and myself. It was a partnership at that stage. All the major decisions were made by Jimmy and me. We knew that if we couldn't agree, there was no decision. We worked fine together: initially we tripped over each other, but eventually we learned not to. He was interested in ordering books, and the quality of the books that we had, and he wasn't really interested in anything outside the South Bridge shop. I took on the responsibility for the general management that he wasn't actually so keen on: the financial side, and the accounting side, and things like stationery, and science, and the music department. So we could actually go on saying hello to each other in the corridor for a week or two, mostly not treading on each other's toes, each looking after their own areas.

Jimmy was an impossible person to fight with on any permanent basis. You could really have serious arguments with Jimmy, because he and I were like oil and water, totally different sorts – which was probably one of the advantages. You could have real bust-ups with him, and then he would come back half an hour later saying, 'So what are you going to do for a holiday, this year?' It was very difficult to have a real disagreement with him permanently, and we didn't, and we enjoyed the thirty-two years working together.

Jimmy had a good sense of humour, and was slightly eccentric, but in a very nice way. He was basically very interested in the quality of books, and very concerned with the quality of books we had in our shop, and also that were being published. He was involved in a lot of the buying at that stage, because when I first joined, almost all the buying was done by Uncle Ainslie, and then later on by Jimmy. Other people were allowed to help a bit, but not too much. We changed this gradually as we got bigger, and we had to spread the responsibility. But at that stage, it was done by one of the partners. So Jimmy was involved in the buying, particularly in the academic department, and he got very involved in the secondhand and antiquarian department later on, when we lost our main antiquarian buyer. He was an enthusiast for books, which was good, and he was concerned with the quality of books in our shop.

But he was an eccentric. He bought some of his clothes from Oxfam for home use, with trousers held up by a string. He had a very old waterproof that he used to wear, and one night I was phoned up by the police saying that an old tramp had been seen breaking into our shop. So I rushed down there, and the police and I searched the building and there was no-one there at all. I had my suspicions, and the next morning I asked Jimmy, 'Did you come into the shop last night?' And he said, 'Oh yes, I just popped in for five minutes to pick something up' – this 'something' was his old raincoat. It appears that a member of the public had identified him as a tramp. When some years later he retired, I gave him a new raincoat, which I'm sure he never wore.

EXPANSION

I was a scientist, and therefore I believed in facts and sums, finding out the information and making decisions. Certainly, I was interested in expanding the business, which Jimmy really wasn't. He was quite happy to remain in South Bridge. I went off to Australia on a trip to talk to Australians about book clubs. While I was out there, I met a number of the Australian booksellers, and it was a very interesting experience for me. It made me feel that we should be expanding our business, not just sitting there with what we had.

When I came back, I heard from one of the reps that a business in Inverness was for sale. I started getting interested, and went up to have a look at it. We eventually bought it [Melven's Bookshop in Inverness]. I remember it was a very exciting time: it was the first significant thing that we had bought. We spent £93,000 on it, which was an enormous amount of money for us in those days: the bidding went up, and we put in an offer, and we had to increase it, and increase it a bit more, and eventually we did get it. It was actually a very successful investment. We expanded that shop seven times, I think, by buying the space around it, and it became by far the biggest and the best bookshop in the north of Scotland and had a great reputation. It has been rather overtaken by the existence of Waterstone's, but for a significant amount of time it was the best bookshop in the north of Scotland.

We then opened another smaller shop in Aviemore, largely because our family used to go there on holiday, and we thought it might be useful to have a shop in the new centre that was opening up. That was a success for a while, but it became less successful as the Aviemore Centre reduced in importance, so we moved it over to the village, and it's still there now. We opened up in Perth and then in Newcastle. Later we closed Newcastle, because it didn't do very well, and we amalgamated the Melven shops with James Thin.

Meanwhile, we'd also expanded James Thin. We'd bought the Edinburgh Bookshop as it was called then in 1981. We had to pay over £1 million for it, so the sums were getting bigger. That shop had been running at a loss, and we had our plans, and it was interesting to see that these plans did, more or less, work out. Malcolm Gibson, who'd been running our general South Bridge shop, went in as manager. He and I spent the first three months there when between us we closed down the old ticket office, closed down the secondhand department, expanded the book department considerably, and refitted the stationery department. My wife went into the coffee room, which was a waitress-service operation, and she changed that to self-service. My two daughters, who were on school holiday at the time – this was about June – went in and helped in the coffee room. From making a loss, it became one of the most profitable parts, percentage-wise, in the shop, and the whole shop was making really good money within a couple of years.

That was an encouraging move, and we went on to open up academic shops: one in St Andrews, at Heriot–Watt University, and at King's Buildings [University of Edinburgh], and we'd already opened up at Buccleuch Street, which was our social sciences bookshop. We went on to open general shops in Dundee and Ayr, and to take over one in Dumfries, and then the last major expansion was in 1992, the purchase of the Volume One chain, which consisted of twenty bookshops. After that, in the mid-1990s, we had a turnover of about £37 million and about 650 staff. Profits peaked at just over £900,000. The Net Book Agreement went three years after we bought Volume One, which was a serious factor, because that brought supermarkets in to sell a lot of the best-selling books, which affected the Volume One bookshops in particular. That was a slippery slope from which it was not possible to escape. If the economics of an industry change, there are casualties – there always are. In every field, you can see that happening in lots of retail businesses.

So at the end of the day the competition affected our sales and our profitability, and the general shops were sold to Ottakar's, and the academic to Blackwell's [of Oxford]. At one stage we were the third or fourth largest bookshop chain in the UK, and we were very important in Scotland, because we had so many bookshops in Scotland and also sold a lot of Scottish books.

SCOTTISHNESS AND BOOKSELLING
I think the Scottish publishers felt we were pretty support-ive of their efforts, because Scottish books sell well, and you would really be silly to have a bookshop in Scotland and not make a serious effort to sell Scottish books. We also felt that this was an obligation on our part, that if we were going to run bookshops in Scotland we would do something about promoting good Scottish books. People who work in bookshops are not there because they are getting paid a lot of money (because that is not usually the case) – a lot of them are there because they really do like books, and are interested in books, and they want to promote the books as well. There were a lot of people in our bookshop chain who were very interested in Scottish books and had a real, genuine love of the bookselling business.

STOCK MANAGEMENT AND COMPUTERS
In the early days when we opened up new shops, the manager was left to run the thing. A lot of the ordering was done by them: sometimes all the ordering was done by them in the shop. We expanded and got into computer systems. As a result of the PA consultancy that we had

undertaken in 1964/65, we started using computers, and we were the first retail bookshop in the UK to do this. At that time we were preparing punch tape in the shop and sending that to a computer bureau that was run by a big computer company in St Andrews Square, and getting back from that orders for publishers and for books, and statements for customers, saying how much they owed us. That was a pretty difficult way of organising things, but nevertheless it was a step forward at the time and a step towards more effective financial management. We had a very difficult eighteen-month period when we set it up, but after that it worked quite well for about fourteen years.

We then moved on to having our own computers. We got a firm called AE Data Services. I knew the chap who set it up, and we were his first customer. I very much told them what we wanted, and they wrote the programmes for us. That lasted for about another ten years, and then we upgraded. By that time we were getting onto the system every book that was sold: its ISBN was being recorded on the till, and then at the end of each day or the [next] morning, each department, or someone in a shop, could just go through all the sales and the books of the previous day and see how many had been sold, how many were in stock, how many to order and how many had sold in the last little while. You could automatically and very quickly go through this and reorder accurately. It became more and more simple as the computer system became more complex. A lot of this was done in the early stages with – not punch tape, we'd moved on from that – but sheets and sheets of computer printout which you had to go through and read. But at the end of the day, we had a very slick system, doing nearly everything on-screen.

I had heard about a program called D-Base, so when

we bought the shop in Newcastle, or just before that, I looked at D-Base II, and decided that I would be able to write programs with this. This was something I did at lunchtimes or in the evenings, so when we opened up the bookshop in Newcastle we used this system. They recorded everything on the tills; the till rolls were sent up to head office; the data was entered into a computer; and then we reordered stock on the basis of these sales. Soon the sales data came up to us over the telephone line. That system was refined quite a lot, and eventually twenty-seven of our bookshops were run on this D-Base system that was very suitable for us. I think a lot of bookshop systems are now based on this same method of recording sales, and reordering, so when you do reorder, you can see on the screen what the situation is for the title. It means you can replace books that are maybe selling once every three months. You do keep the breadth of stock, but you don't have too much stock, which is very expensive, obviously. We were the first retail bookseller to use computers, and they became very important to us in the control of stock and of the business, as they have done for most bookshops now.

BOOK-TRADE REPS

The publisher's rep used to be very important. When I joined the business there was very little stock control. Major books that were selling well would, of course, be reordered as it was noticed that they were needed – and the staff were very good at noticing. Our stock control in the academic department consisted of an exercise book, where we wrote down how many copies of a particular book you had sold in the previous year. But there wasn't good stock control of the new general books that were coming in, of the paperbacks, or of the backlist. So the reps would come in and take stock and say, 'Well, you should be having this', and we'd say, 'Well, I want that', and they would come in quite regularly, say once a month, from all the big publishers. So you'd reorder stock that way, which is terribly inefficient, because it means you could go out of stock of something in the first few days of the month, and you wouldn't reorder until the end of the month. When computers came in, and you were given the opportunity to reorder almost immediately, it was much, much more efficient. The number of reps has declined since then, and they felt that they have been a threatened species, but there still are some around, and they now arrange for special deals and promotions for bookshops. But because so many of the booksellers now are in big chains, a lot can be done centrally in one office.

We tried to restrict the reps to some extent, because it made no sense to us for, say, fifty reps to be going in to our bookshops, all of them taking up two hours of time, with one of our most expensive people, and then duplicating this throughout the empire, so we tended to do a lot of ordering centrally. Not everyone liked it, but it was a fairly efficient way of dealing with it. With big English publishers we tended to subscribe centrally and reorder through our computer system, and that was done centrally through our head office. But the individual shops tended to have a fair amount of freedom in ordering local or Scottish books.

FAMILY BUSINESS

Up to a certain point in time, personnel issues were just dealt with by Jimmy and myself, but then my daughter Hilary joined us and she took on quite a lot of the staffing matters. She was very good at motivating people. Later on, my other daughter Jackie joined us. She was a qualified accountant, and she took on the personnel responsibility. She obtained a qualification in personnel management. Up to that point we'd dealt with problems as they arose, and if we wanted advice we would get lawyers or whatever. But once Jackie arrived on the scene, things were dealt with systematically. We had a proper personnel policy, and we dealt with things in a more professional manner.

Then my son Jamie came in to look after our computers. After taking a degree in physics and computing, he did a teaching qualification and spent a year teaching in Pakistan. He taught in England for a bit, did a further course in Glasgow on computers and then joined us. He was with us for about four or five years. Actually one of the first things he did was take charge of the Gyle shop for the first eighteen months when we first opened up there, which he very much enjoyed and which was very successful. Then he came to the main shop when we bought Volume One, because suddenly we had to get new computer systems into twenty new bookshops. So he came in to help us do that.

Jimmy and I made Thin's a limited company in the '70s, so we then had to have directors. Initially, Jimmy and I were the only directors, but then later on we appointed other directors and we then had proper regular board meetings. We also had staff meetings every Tuesday morning in each shop. A memo would be sent to the person who was running the staff meeting and the board's views presented to the staff at that time. So all the shops would be doing this on a Tuesday. We'd explain, for example, that we'd just bought Volume One, or that we were going to handle this matter differently and the reasons why, and the manager would be there explaining why it was going to happen. The managers were brought together twice a year; there was a lot to discuss on the agenda.

Remodelling South Bridge

When I first joined the business there were lots of small rooms, and we gradually reduced the number of these eventually by knocking down walls. The first thing I remember is that we built two floors on the back of the old dispatch area, and that became our mail-order department and our accounts department. They were quite big floors. Then, later on, as we withdrew from mail order to a certain extent because it was unprofitable, we were able to transfer our academic department to one of those rooms, and the other one was used for an extension of our general book department. The secondhand department, when I joined the business, took up 30 per cent of the space and provided about 5 per cent of the turnover. It took up the whole basement area. We changed that eventually, and brought the children's department down to the basement, and that enabled us to extend it a lot.

Thin's employees

[For years] Elizabeth Granger presided over the children's department. She had been there since the 1950s. When I joined in 1957/58 she was there, but she died in the late 1960s. She certainly was the very best children's bookseller that we had in the business, and she was very well known. Often when you met people they didn't say, 'Oh, you're from James Thin'; they'd say, 'I know Elizabeth Granger – she runs that fantastic children's department.' So it was one of the best-known departments in the shop, and rightly so, because Elizabeth was a total enthusiast, and it was very difficult to get her out of the shop. Jimmy and I had to frequently practically throw her out when it reached 7.30 at night, because she was never anxious to leave.

She had a remarkable facility. She read a lot of the books, so she really knew what was in them. She had a terrific memory. She did it with our children; she also did it with lots of other people's children. I remember she'd say, 'Ah, you read that last time, so now you are ready for this', and she did this with hundreds and hundreds of people. They all thought that she was doing something special for them – which she was, in a way. She had her favourite books; she hated Enid Blyton. If Jimmy and I hadn't insisted, she would have had no Enid Blyton in the shop at all. We pointed out that you really had to, because some people learnt to read with Enid Blyton, and then they got quickly fed up with it and moved onto better material. Anyhow, Elizabeth didn't like it. She was a great character and enormously liked by her customers. She died at the age of fifty-two. She was a very heavy smoker, and you have to assume it was something to do with that. It was very sad; she should have been with us a great deal longer.

I remember there was Jimmy Burnett, who was in charge of the dispatch department when I joined. He was quite a character. I think he spent all his working life in the business. I quickly discovered that if Jimmy wasn't happy, the whole shop was unhappy, because somehow he managed to get everyone upset. So as soon as I discovered that, I made it my purpose that, if nothing else, Jimmy Burnett was happy! You had to give him a bottle of whisky at New Year. My uncle started that practice and I continued it. But you also had to know how to deal with him, and if he had a reasonable gripe, then you dealt with it. If you sorted out a fairly minor issue, then end of story! Everyone was happy again.

Then there was a chap called Peter Watson in our general book department. I remember well him telling me about his early days in the Douglas & Foulis shop in Castle Street, because he'd been an apprentice and worker there for a long time. At that stage it was a very upmarket bookshop. Ladies would arrive in chauffeur-driven cars that would stop outside, and the lady would come in. The main manager was allowed to speak to the customers and no-one else was. All the other bookshop workers were parked round the shop, like the fielders in a cricket match. So if the manager discovered that the lady was interested in gardening, he would click his fingers and the person who was in charge of gardening would rush across with the latest two or three books, and if it was sport [click], someone else would come forward – and if it was fiction [click], and so on. So they would all come forward, and these offerings would be presented to the lady, who would make her selection and then get back into her Rolls Royce and drive off again. It was a rather interesting vision of how bookselling took place in the '30s. Peter was with us for a long time and was a very important person in our front shop and knew the customers very well. One American who hadn't been in the shop for I think fifteen or twenty years stepped inside the shop, and Peter Watson said, 'Hello Professor so-and-so' and the chap was suitably impressed, as you can imagine.

THEFT

Theft was always a very significant problem – when we were at our largest, I think we were losing about £1 million a year in theft, which is rather upsetting, but you have to bear in mind that no retail business can open its doors without losing something in theft. The solution of closing your doors is not entirely satisfactory! So you've got to just limit it, which is what we did. We tried various methods of tagging books, but it was never very successful, and it never could be 100 per cent successful. The other thing, of course, is that you've got a very few of your own staff stealing from you by taking money out of the till. There were quite a few incidents of that. We introduced a firm to make sample purchases – you have to do that if you are in retailing – and the first person we caught we all liked very much. She admitted to stealing a bit of money at first to buy some fags on Friday, and she was busy buying a car when we caught her!

INVOLVEMENT IN PUBLISHING
Oliver and Boyd [Edinburgh publisher] was bought jointly in about 1900 by the Thins and John Grant – they were the secondhand booksellers on George IV Bridge. The most important thing [produced by Oliver and Boyd] was its educational publishing series called the Happy Venture Readers, which was used very widely in the UK, and in Australia and the West Indies. It also had a scientific list, a Scottish list and a theological list that Jimmy started up. It was a pretty successful business. But in 1962, one of my uncles who had a lot of the shares was Uncle Tommy. If he had died, there would have been death duties of around £100,000 to pay, which was a lot of money in those days, and the money wasn't available within the family. You can't easily sell one sixth of a publishing business, so we were advised by the accountant, Professor David Anderson, that we should sell Oliver and Boyd, which we did, to the *Financial Times*. So that was the end of that adventure in publishing. I was very young at the time but, personally, I think it was a big mistake, looking back. If the decision could be taken again, I would have wanted to find another solution. Unfortunately, it meant the end of an important

Children's Room, John Smith & Son, Glasgow *(Robert Clow)*

Second-hand Department, Basement, John Smith & Son, Glasgow *(Robert Clow)*

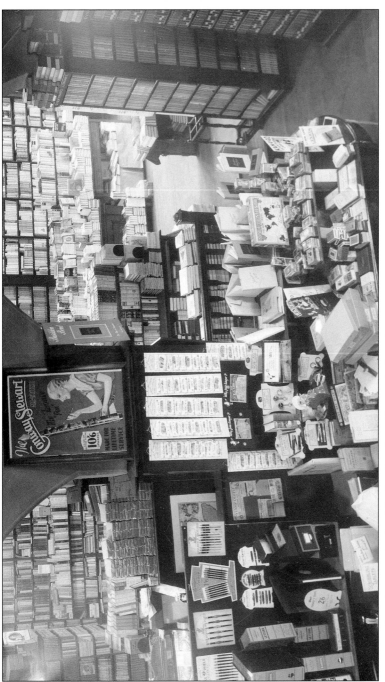

Stationery through to new books, John Smith & Son, Glasgow *(Robert Clow)*

Recital at John Smith & Son, Glasgow (*Robert Clow*)

Stirling University Bookshop, John Smith & Son, Glasgow (*Robert Clow*)

Bauermeister Bookshop at 19 West Regent Street Glasgow c.1910 *(Bill Bauermeister)*

Ainslie Thin in the South Bridge bookshop *(Ainslie Thin)*

Margaret Squires in the Quarto Bookshop, St Andrews *(Jennie Renton)*

Scottish publishing house – it used to publish a lot of important Scottish books. But it just gradually disappeared from the scene completely. It was really sad.

Jimmy and I started up the Mercat Press a few years later, in 1970. We started it up not because we expected to make much money out of it, but we'd knocked the bookselling business into shape and were in pretty good financial shape. We did it on the basis initially of republishing a number of classic Scottish books. Mostly they were chosen by Jimmy from the antiquarian side. He just came up with the things he knew were in considerable demand that he thought we could sell. Some of them were Oliver and Boyd reprints like *Edinburgh's Child* [*Some Memories of Ninety Years*] by [Eleanor] Sillar [1979], which was quite a bestseller in its time, and Lord Cockburn's *Circuit Journeys*, and Burns, *Studies of Poems and Songs, St Kilda* [*A Voyage to St Kilda* by Martin Martin, 1970], and the *Edinburgh History of Scotland* [edited by Gordon Donaldson in four volumes].

Then we started publishing original books. There was *An Edinburgh Alphabet* [J. F. Birrell, 1980], which was one of the first, and 'Campaigns of Montrose' [*A Military History of the Civil War in Scotland* by Stuart Reid, 1990], *Mary Stewart's People* by [Margaret] Sanderson [1987], *The Romans in Scotland* by Gordon Maxwell [1989], and so on. Later we bought other lists from publishers who were going out of business for one reason or another. Most of Aberdeen University Press came our way. At that time, we set up our separate editorial department as a proper publishing department, which Tom Johnson and Sean Costello worked in, and they gradually took over the whole publishing business, which up to that time Jimmy and I had been looking after in our spare time. An excellent person called Tom

Jenkins, who used to work for Oliver and Boyd, we used as a designer. He used to lay it all out, had the jacket design organised, and so on. So it was a fairly simple operation, which may not have been all that exciting. But it worked quite well. And then we bought some books from Her Majesty's Stationery Office, so it became quite a big business, and it publishes twenty, twenty-five books a year now.

EXPANDING THE BUSINESS

I was interested in expanding the business, so I remember the enormous excitement when we first bought the shop in Inverness, and each time we took a step like this I found it quite exhilarating. Buying the Edinburgh Bookshop was another such instance. We opened up a new shop in Dundee, on a site found by Andrew Thin and Derek Gordon (a surveyor), and the Gyle shop was another interesting one, because the rent we had to pay there was very high at about £95,000 – it was in a new shopping centre and we didn't really know how it was going to work. You can do sums, but we had very few facts. Eventually we decided to go in, and I knew it had to achieve a turnover of £800,000 a year to break even. In fact, it finished up by doing well over £2 million [a year]. So it was very successful, but it might not have been. We did open up in Newcastle, which seemed a good idea at the time, but it wasn't really, and we had to withdraw from there. So – you win some, you lose some. But being involved in these decisions was very exciting, and I just enjoyed being involved in books, and with books, and in expanding the business. I never found the book trade boring: there are always new books coming in, some of them very exciting – new series, new imprints – and you are in the middle of something that is always changing.

WORKING WITH AUTHORS

We had lots of publisher's parties that one would get invited to; sometimes nice private little dinners where you would be sitting beside authors. I sat next to Anita Shreve at an authors' event. I admired her books, and it was great to have a chat with her. These sorts of events were very enjoyable. I felt very privileged to be involved in them. Many Edinburgh authors had connections with our shop, like Dorothy Dunnett, because we used to advertise her books on the internet, and when she produced her new book we used to sell several hundred through that method. She would come in and sign the copies and we would send them to customers, many of them in America, and we certainly were involved in quite a number of author sessions with her. Ian Rankin has always been supportive of us, and we of him, I think. So he has been involved with us in lots of events. J. K. Rowling wrote the first book in that little coffee shop just round the corner [from the South Bridge shop]. We sold that book well, right from the beginning. But then, she was a local author, and we've always sold local authors well. But it took a lot longer for her books to become the international best-sellers that they are now. Alexander McCall Smith, the author who wrote the *Number One Detective Agency* books, launched his first adult book with us. I remember Hilary organised the launch party, and he brought all his friends along, a party for two or three hundred people – it was a great success and we sold maybe four or five hundred of that book. But it only became a bestseller six or seven years later.

THE END OF JAMES THIN BOOKSELLERS

The end happened very quickly, but we knew there had been problems for some time. The first factor that caused our closure was the growth of the chains – Waterstone's and people like that. They were opening bookshops in places where we were functioning. Ottakar's came in and opened up lots of bookshops, and then Borders was opening vast new bookshops also. That was a real problem. Bookshops opening up near our existing branches made our shops less profitable, or actually pushed them into a loss.

Then the Net Book Agreement collapsed in 1995. That was very significant. It didn't change things immediately, but it did change them gradually, because the supermarkets came in and started selling popular books. They liked to have books that they could discount and weren't terribly interested until they could discount. But after the loss of the NBA, they moved from having 2 per cent of the home market for books to about 12 per cent, which is a colossal change. That was all in the popular end of the trade – Dick Francis, Wilbur Smith, that type of thing. That had a particular effect on the Volume One shops [owned by Thin's in England] because they, more than our other shops, tended to concentrate on the popular end of the general market. So we started having trouble. I think if the NBA had held we could have made the Volume One purchase work. We then had to start closing down some of the Volume One shops as they became unprofitable, and that is not always easy. You can't always get rid of a shop when you want to; you have to always carry the loss for longer than you would wish. So we found ourselves on a slippery slope – books weren't supplying enough turnover to keep the whole thing going – and we tried terribly hard to increase sales by putting in other items like jigsaws and stationery items. We put a great effort into that, but it didn't work. As fast as you increased your sales of jigsaws, you slightly decreased your sales of books, because on the whole people like pure bookshops and don't like them watered down with lots of other things. But we couldn't just sit on our hands and just do nothing, so we had to try that. Eventually, when we realised that the various measures we were taking weren't working, that was when we had to go into administration. This was certainly encouraged by the bank, because we still had a loan from the bank at this stage. We'd borrowed £4.5 million to buy Volume One and still had £1.9 million outstanding. At the end of the day, all the people that we owe money to will get their money back. The final result has been 97.9 pence in the pound – they'll have given us a very small extra discount on their last few invoices, which after 154 years is not such a price to pay. Most of the people who go into administration pay virtually nothing.

It's not nice that it happened, and it's very, very sad for us, because a lot of people worked very, very hard for something that we thought was worthwhile. You had to just see the amount of effort that went into avoiding the sale of James Thin. I was very aware of the pressure on our management team. They were working all hours – having meetings at all hours on what was to be done – and I don't think anything else could have been done. It was a colossal effort, and eventually you had to face up to the fact that the bits that had to be sold needed to be sold, and the best way to do that was through administration; that way the business can be kept running, and you have time to run things down in an orderly manner.

The end was due to a number of things. The purchase of the Volume One chain in England would have worked if the Net Book Agreement hadn't gone – and to be fair, there is still a net book agreement, or something close to it, in Germany and in France, and in the UK the Net Book Agreement had been operating since 1900. So it had been there for ninety-four years, and it could well be there now if it hadn't been given away by four major players – such as W. H. Smith, who decided it could do without it, and three major publishers. But we weren't to know that that was to happen. But I think it was the growth of the chains – that was the most important factor, actually. The Net Book Agreement was the next important factor. And, yes, looking back, if we hadn't bought Volume One we would have been in better shape, but I still think that we would have lost out, because we would not have been big enough, really. The purchase of Volume One immediately increased our margins by about 2 per cent, because we increased our sales from £17 million to £37 million. We suddenly became a very big operation and were able to increase our margins for the whole business. I think that because of the change in economics, our number was probably up whatever happened – I don't think it would be easy to avoid it.

I think our last opportunity for selling the business came in the late 1980s. If we'd sold it then we could have probably sold it at a reasonable price. But at that time we were growing fast, we were profitable, we were doing well, we were running a business that we liked, enjoyed and were proud of, and the last thing in the world that would have crossed our minds was selling the business then, although it would have been a good business decision if you'd been able to make that decision ice-cold.

CONCLUSION

I certainly enjoyed being involved in the business, and I enjoyed going around the bookshops and meeting the managers on a regular basis, which I did in the early days when we started building up branches. I think everyone just felt that they were doing something worthwhile. In

most cases, you see, we were putting in the best bookshop
in the town. In Dundee we opened up a shop that was
better than anything they'd had before. In Ayr, the same.
In Dumfries, we took over a bookshop and made it a better
bookshop. In Inverness we took over a very small bookshop
and made it into a very big one. Likewise, in Edinburgh,
we had South Bridge and George Street, the two best
bookshops in Edinburgh by far. We were a quality bookseller and proud of that fact.

Bill Bauermeister

A FAMILY BUSINESS

My German grandfather was a bookseller who had left Hanover in his twenties. He had trained there in bookselling and then he went to work in Paris. He worked for a company with which I later dealt when I was a young man, Librairie Klincksieck, a French publisher and bookseller; you know the distinction wasn't always very clear in those days. It used to provide beautiful copperplate invoices – even in my day. From Paris he went to work in London, again in bookselling, and he eventually landed up in Glasgow, where he seems to have bought out in 1916 Wilson Ross, who were successors to Otto Schulze in 1900. He appears in Glasgow in the 1891 census. He may have been there before that, but that locates him there. He was selling books in his own right under his own name in Glasgow before the turn of the [twentieth] century. He was a 'foreign bookseller' who spoke English with a German guttural accent. He married a Glasgow lady and proceeded to produce eight children – one of whom, the second eldest, my father, eventually continued in bookselling.

In the meantime, my grandfather had come to Edinburgh to live and opened a business here in Hanover Street, then later at 7 North Bank Street on the Mound, now part of the trustee department of the head office of the Bank of Scotland. That's actually where I started work as a bookseller. The name by which my grandfather traded was F. Bauermeister – 'F' for Friedrich. That was the name above the door on the Mound: 'F. Bauermeister, Foreign Bookseller'. He traded right through the Second World War. I have only recently unearthed evidence of this. I've been doing research in the *Scotsman* digital archives: searching for 'Bauermeisters' produced fascinating evidence showing he was advertising right in the middle of Edinburgh in the middle of the war! Quite bold, but he was very secure, it seems, in the Edinburgh environment. However, he grew senile during the Second World War. In 1943 the business was sold to Sir Will Y. Darling, former lord provost of Edinburgh and author, coincidentally, of *The Private Papers of a Bankrupt Bookseller* in 1931. His reason for buying the business, as he explained himself, was that he spent more time in Grant's bookshop next door to his haberdashery in Princes Street than he did in his own business!

My aunt, my father's younger sister Janette, ran the business for a period towards the end of the war for Will Y. Darling. I've recently found interesting evidence of joint advertising after the war in the *Scotsman*: Darling's and Grant's and Bauermeister's – advertising 'three high-quality businesses'. My father had been serving as a Royal Signals officer for six years of the war, four of them in the Middle East. At the end of the war, he came back and wanted to do architecture, but he had a sprog – me, only one, born in 1937 – and a wife to support. He had to get a job and found one as Will Y. Darling's managing director in the bookshop on the Mound. It still had 'F. Bauermeister' above the door. My father did very well and clearly also got on well with Will Y. Darling, because eventually Darling came to our house at least a couple of times for dinner. My father and he used to enjoy a good whisky. I think Darling was very happy to sell the business back to my father.

At the Royal High School where I went to school and sat my Highers in 1955, you had to stay on at school until the very bitter end – you weren't allowed to leave after the exams without good reason. My father told a downright lie to the school, saying that I was coming into the business. There was no intention of my coming into the business. My father had bought a site off Bonaly Road in Colinton on which to build a house, and I was to be his labourer. So my first contribution to the book trade was as a builder's labourer. My father had a bankrupt builder, a Mr Ellis, as my boss, and we worked there during the day. My father finished work at night on the Mound and would come home, and with a pal of his, whom *he* later helped build *his* house, they carried on building at night. The house was built, and after five or six years the house was sold in order to buy back the business. At that point we had a connection with the Dean Hotel in Clarendon Crescent, and we got a very cheap deal there. We stayed in the Dean Hotel for a while until my parents could find another house. And that's how the business came back into family possession in 1960.

I remember going into the shop as a youngster. I remember things like the old cash register that we actually had on the premises until I sold the business in 1999. As a child, it was a wonderful thing, you know. Then there were the typewriters, or 'trypeaters' as they were called in the business – old-fashioned, great heavy things, they were wonderful toys, unbreakable by children. I remember the mustiness of the bookshop. The books were 90 per cent new, but the smell came from the premises: the wood panelling and some fine, old, glass-covered cases in which we kept the serious art books: the complete range of Skira monographs on the great artists, the great painters. Art was our other main specialisation; I reckon we were the best source of art books in Scotland. There was a reservoir of knowledge about these subjects, too, in the people who worked there.

APPRENTICESHIP

After National Service and a bit of university, I think I was probably, not inspired, hardly inspired, but attracted to the business for the reason that there was already a kind of total family commitment. My father had devoted everything to the business. We had British books, but the specialisation was foreign books. When I joined the company, that was the interesting part for me. I wasn't particularly interested in selling British books – that wasn't the real work; researching foreign books was much, much more interesting for me and was one of the main draws to the business. When I went into the business I was regarded very differently: as a young whip-persnapper, an upstart, to be kept in line. My father had a wonderful servant, a Mrs Traube, who was German. Her husband had been murdered by the Nazis – he had been a scientist – and she lived alone in Edinburgh, in Morningside. She just worked assiduously for my father, and I suppose in a way worshipped him. So when I came into the business eventually at the age of twenty-three or so, I became a wedge between them, I guess, and she didn't really like what I was doing. But I knew that I was doing the right thing; my father was a very, very good teacher and the business at this time was developing in a most interesting way.

The deal with my father was that I would serve an apprenticeship. I was interested in languages, quite good at them. The original deal was then that I was to spend six months each in France, Germany, Holland, probably, and in Italy, probably – but that was to be agreed later – and I would do an apprenticeship period in Edinburgh with Ian Grant, the antiquarian bookseller, because that was a skill not actually held within the family. That was the idea, but it didn't quite come about like that. The actuality was that I did go to France, and I had a wonderful time working for the *département étranger* of Hachette on the Boulevard Saint-Germain, on the corner of Saint-Michel. I earned an apprentice's wage in Paris and was subsidised to his limited ability by my father as well.

I learned a lot in what was actually the export department. I would see all the new books in France and know what was selling in France and relate it to what *I* thought we could sell in Edinburgh, which was a bit bumptious really. I would just pass these books into our *cases* [pigeonholes]. Every customer had such boxes on the walls, and books would be piled into them as they came from the publishers. Eventually the *dactylo* [typist], Denise Couhault, would use this very fancy machine to get an invoice out and send the books out to Edinburgh. My poor father and Frank Carroll, the very talented linguist, had to sell the damn things. I was buying them, and as you know it's the easiest thing to buy books: the more difficult thing is to sell the blasted things. I was effectively stocking up our tiny shop, with insufficient headroom on the lower floor, with French books. But this fitted the business picture; my father's strategy was that we would persevere with the foreign business.

When I was in Paris theoretically studying my apprenticeship, I received messages indirectly from my father. My father only had a staff of three and a cleaner – that was it, and here was I, swanning about Paris, learning to be a French bookseller. The messages received were 'hmm, it's costing money to keep you there', and 'there's a heck of a lot of work to be done here'. So eventually, off my own back, I saw the director who was responsible for me in Hachette and said: 'I think I ought to go home. I think there's work to be done there.' I had sown the wild oats there, so to speak, and got back to Edinburgh and got stuck in.

I had actually shared a flat with two Scots accountants near Place Clichy in Paris. These two chaps were very well paid. I was an apprentice. My contribution to the flat was financially very small by comparison. These guys were groundbreaking. There were very few chartered accountants. The French had their own qualification, but it wasn't as good as the Scottish CA in its professional training. Scots accountants were hugely in demand. In fact my uncle, my father's youngest brother, George, only six years older than me, became the senior partner for Deloitte in Europe, working out of Paris, where he still lives. A year or two after leaving Paris, I was back. I was going to Germany by car and had booked a night with my former flatmate, by then married and still living and working as an accountant in Paris. And I met my wife there! She was on her way back from Turkey, where she'd been working as a nursery nurse. So our paths crossed there in Paris and we married in 1962.

University Sales

The British universities had all been deprived of much periodical and book literature, of course, during the war period and now suddenly [at the beginning of the 1960s] they were being funded with loads of money to balance, as it were, the money going into the new universities that were being created. They had to spend all this by the end of their budget period. My father would be on holiday – and this is where Mrs Traube and I would fall out. I was young and gallus and got on with it and did it; that was what she really objected to. St Andrews University would phone up, Glasgow would phone up, Aberdeen would phone up, Edinburgh would phone up, Newcastle would phone up, and say, 'Please, could you send us invoices for back-runs of the following journals.' I would ask 'For how much?' and I would make up, in a sense, phoney invoices, because we hadn't supplied the goods and didn't *know* that we could supply the goods for, at that time, *thousands* of pounds in the early 1960s. My father would come back and say: 'Fine, you've done rather well.' But of course we had to find these back-runs. In Europe in particular, and in the United States of America as well, there were one or two very smart printing houses doing photomechanical reprints of back-runs of academic jour- nals and of some books. We became British experts on these sources. You couldn't look up the internet in those days: you had to know, you would have had to have seen them, you had to go there.

So we were a real reservoir, only later recognised, of unique knowledge. There were lists circulated, and librarians were gaily phoning us up: 'Send us invoices for £1,000, please' – a huge amount of money at the time. That was quite fun. But then of course we had to research them and actually get them. And we *did*. That was the very, very interesting bit of the business, for me – for the number of years that it lasted. Eventually, of course, the universities had their library funds pulled back in, and reality was restored. But they were necessary, those journals. They were accessed across the faculties really, in arts and sciences, but obviously the sciences got priority. Academics needed to know what had been going on over a period for which that resource of information was not available to them in the libraries. Other booksellers didn't have the foreign connections in places like Holland, Switzerland and the United States of America.

ENTER CAPTAIN MAXWELL

Our location on the Mound, we recognised, was far too small for what we actually wanted to do. We were aware that we'd have to find somewhere else sometime. But there wouldn't be the financial resources; there was no family money or anything like that. The money my father had made, enough to buy the business, had been by virtue of selling our house. So we had a requirement to find larger premises, and then a strange thing happened. Captain I. R. Maxwell appeared on the Scottish scene: Robert Maxwell – himself a brilliant linguist. However, in about 1965, he appeared in Scotland in a way that worried us. I should say that by this time our journal-subscription business dominated the firm. It was not only the photomechanical reproductions and not only our specialism in current foreign publications: we were also journal subscription specialists in a way that dated back to the type of trade my grandfather had plied in Glasgow, and later my father. They used to sell the important fashion magazines to the Jewish tailoring trade, which was very important in Glasgow. All the Glasgow women were better dressed than the Edinburgh women, needless to say! Tailoring was a very important industry in Glasgow. It was because of that they would sell *Elle* and *Vogue* when these were big names.

When the Spring and Autumn Collection issues appeared, each fetched a huge price; and if they appeared today at the prices pertaining then, I mean they might be £25 or £50 each. So that started a subscription business, way back. It developed in the meantime into the academic journal subscription business, and we were very, very keyed in to the – particularly Scottish – universities for that. So when the university libraries phoned up for photomechanical reproductions or back-runs, they were already dealing with us as regular suppliers of journals and books. So they knew our competence on that front.

We had very strong connections with all the Scottish universities through our journal subscriptions service. These were the old universities, not Stirling and the later newer ones. It gave us an avenue to university libraries that other booksellers would have had to work hard to get into. We could speak to the right people. Out of the blue, Robert Maxwell and his company, the Pergamon Press, arrived on the scene. Maxwell had been a British army officer during the war and just post-war. Before an exchange rate had been set up officially by the British government with Germany, he did a deal with Herr Springer of Springer Verlag [the large German publishing house] in Berlin at an exchange rate *he* had fixed. Then when the official exchange rate was actually announced – I don't know the precise details – but within, it seems to me, a month or two, Maxwell was already making 100 per cent profit, just on the difference between his agreed exchange rate and the official one. Springer was the most important academic publisher in the world, because he published chemistry and physics out of Germany; that knowledge was wanted here and in the United States of America. I even believe that my German grandfather *was* allowed to import particular publications from Germany during the war, including Springer serial publications such as Gmelin's *Handbuch der anorganischen Chemie* and the equivalent *Handbuch der Physik*. When I was dealing with them in the 1960s, still servicing them after very many years, when they came in through our hands they were perhaps £100 a volume. These were very serious, important academic works of limited circulation. I have an understanding that their import was allowed to continue by special licence to my grandfather during part of the Second World War.

However, that was also the market that Maxwell had focused on very, very intelligently. He was a sharp businessman – among many other things! He saw the opportunity and he set up Pergamon Press to service the British universities with these journals. But the way he did it was he made 100 per cent profit on the exchange rate at square one. Then, as was the form with journal subscriptions, he asked the subscriber, the academic library, to pay up front, so he took a year's money in advance – but then his little trick was not to supply the journals for *two* years. He had a lot of money sloshing around, belonging to the British universities. We were a link in that chain, because we acted for the Scottish universities as their journal subscription agents, and we were buying from Maxwell and we were sending the money to Maxwell, and he wasn't supplying. At one point our reputation was, for a small amount of time, on the line, because certainly one university library thought *we* were withholding the money and not supplying the journals. Within a very short space of time, they learned the actual fact: that it was Maxwell.

Now this is the background to the man who appeared

on the Scottish scene in, of all places, Dundee. Maxwell was arriving in Dundee by virtue of trying to buy the academic bookshop there. He also threatened to put in a printing works in Dundee, which he was perfectly capable of doing. The problem, from Dundee's point of view, was that D. C. Thomson was *the* printer. Thomson was strictly non-union, and Maxwell was union, so Thomson didn't like this. Bauermeister's was still operating out of 7 North Bank Street on the Mound, where we had quite a significant business because of journal subscriptions that belied the size and appearance of the shop. This is what Maxwell was impinging on. Maxwell was putting himself in a position in Dundee where he would be very strong with the new university library there, and also in St Andrews, and we had strong interests with both. So my father said: 'Let's see if we can keep him out'. That became a bold thing even to consider.

EXPANDING TO DUNDEE

It was to prevent Maxwell buying that bookshop that my father said: 'I think we should do something about this.' So we went up to Dundee, had a look at the place, and said: 'We'll put in a bid.' However, the lawyers stoked up a bidding war, and eventually my father decided that – his name was Bill, too, by the way – 'This is ridiculous. We're bidding all this for a bookshop. Let *him* buy it and we'll set up next door and compete – because we're better than Maxwell.' We knew a lawyer in Dundee, a young chap, about a year or two older than me at the time, and we said: 'Can you find us a premises in the academic area, please?' This really meant around South Tay Street. This chap went out and actually knocked on doors, stating 'somebody would like to buy . . .'. He phoned us up a few days later, and he said: 'I've found someplace. Can you come up?' My father and I shot up there, and this was an old shop. There was no headroom in its basement, so we had to dig out another five or six feet below. We pulled the place down and rebuilt it.

From the spring of that year, we were open for the new academic year selling medical books and what have you, and displaying Penguins for the first time in Dundee. We had the biggest range of Penguins anywhere, I guess, at that time. And we had a spanking new bookshop. In the meantime, D. C. Thomson, rather powerful in Dundee, had been watching on the sidelines, and *immediately* we showed our hand Thomson stepped in and bought the old bookshop that was for sale because they didn't want Maxwell in – what a relief for us! So, here we were, in Dundee, in our spanking new bookshop, *loving* it. I was managing it from Edinburgh, but I was driving up every morning or so. There was also a good train service at that time. We were carrying books back and forward and really quite enjoying it – although Dundee was a bit of a desert to sell books in, I must say, at that time. We called the shop 'The Tay Street Bookshop' after its location: it was just about underneath the university, actually. I remember I had to go and present myself to the principal [of Dundee University] and say who we were and what we were doing, and what have you. I drove up in auld claes and put on a suit in the car. I remember sweating like a pig! He was very kind to me.

However, here we were in 1965 in competition with people we didn't really want to be in competition with – with D. C. Thomson – who suddenly owned a bookshop too – which they didn't want!

MOVING TO GEORGE IV BRIDGE

My wife and I were going through a homeless period in 1966, with now our first child. The first house we bought was a cottage in Duddingston Village, and it turned out to be riddled with dry rot and woodworm. I spent the next three years rebuilding it myself at nights and at lunchtimes, having fallen back on my training as a builder's labourer. I had the confidence, if not the finance, to do it. We were certainly homeless at one time, for we had to stay with my parents for a short period. I remember one Sunday night my father and I stayed up late, maybe till two in the morning, and got a map of Edinburgh out on the floor in front of the fire, and said: 'Where the heck will we go anyway? Princes Street is too posh, too expensive, and our customers are not there.' Our customers were largely academic, but we also had a mix of people who came across the town, of lawyers and of passing trade, for all of whom the Mound was actually really quite suitable. It was a good site, actually. In those days you could park your car outside the door. It was just that the premises were far too small. We looked at the map, and the cross of 'town and gown' was the sort of expression at the back of our minds. George IV Bridge. Yes, but a pretty dull area: nothing happened on George IV Bridge. Two libraries – very dull-looking in those days. The National Library: not the prettiest architectural edifice. Edinburgh Central Library: a rather dour sort of place in those days. What else was there? The churchy-looking places. So that was it: George IV Bridge would be suitable, but we'd have to work hard at it.

The very next morning, my father and I were driving together to work on the Mound. As the passenger, I was able to look about, and I noticed that the door of the then secondhand bookshop on George IV Bridge was closed. The door was shut, at quarter past nine or whatever time it was. So my father parked the car and he went into our bookshop on the Mound, and I walked back along George IV Bridge and rapped at the door. There was no response. There was a staircase beside it leading to the Scottish Reformation Society above. I didn't know what I was going into, but I went up the stairs and came to a doorway, and here was a lady with a bucket and a mop. 'Can I help you, lad?' she asked. 'Well, actually I was just wondering about the bookshop downstairs. The door's closed.' She said, 'Oh, my husband's not back from the funeral yet.' Her husband was a minister, the Rev. Horne, secretary of the Scottish Reformation Society, and he was actually attending the funeral of the *very* ancient bookseller who had operated there with a camp bed in the shop and a pistol under his pillow. I saw her husband, the man responsible for making the decision whether to sell or not the premises, that same day his previous tenant had been buried! So we secured the property eventually at 19 George IV Bridge, which was to be the main shop, just before the bridge gap over to where the Elephant House is now.

There had been an unwritten understanding with the Bank of Scotland, which was *desperate* to get our premises on the Mound. The bank had said to my father: 'If you ever want to move out, Mr Bauermeister, we'll buy it.' They would pay the top price – there was to be no worry about that. But we couldn't afford to buy 19 George IV Bridge on the strength of just selling that wee shop. We had no other resources except stock. The only other asset we had was the one that we'd created in a very short time from nothing in Dundee. We had just built this spanking new, lovely bookshop, completely fitted out with *the* most modern fittings at the time, and we liked it. Customers liked it. Who was in the market for it? D. C. Thomson. If circumstances had been different, we might have bought *their* bookshop, because we had both to some degree been unwillingly drawn into bookselling in Dundee. Lunch with the responsible director of D. C. Thomson followed – as did an easy deal. They paid us a very good price, so we cleared out. That helped fund the purchase of 19 George IV Bridge. And took us out of Dundee.

BAUERMEISTER BOOKSELLERS, GEORGE IV BRIDGE

The ground floor on George IV Bridge was the highest level; there was one below that, of which initially we had half given over to book stock – the foreign books and the beginnings of the academic book department. The rest was offices. We had two further floors of workshop or cellar space below that, going down to Merchant Street and below. When my father and I were first exploring the place, we took torches, because it was very poorly lit. We found an electric bulb there that was, I think, made by Mr Edison himself! We kept it for years. The premises went under George IV Bridge, and actually into the arches, like the public library. In one of those lower parts of the premises, my father and I were peering in this dark, terrible place, and there was a very low door with a modern padlock on it. We found the right key out of all the keys for the building, opened the door, and we were both bending down to peer through, my father in front of me shining the torch, and here was a lorry! It was the ground floor of somewhere else: the restaurant that used to be on Merchant Street. That's where we were looking through to. There was a truck in there. We had this wee door like Alice in Wonderland,

and behind it a damn great lorry! That was the condition of the place then.

So we opened up on George IV Bridge in 1966. It was still a dreadfully dead place at that time. Mrs Traube transferred with us. She worked for a few years there, before retiring. She was a great servant, to my father in particular: she was a one-man loyal individual; her work was incredibly good. Always. In those days, stocktaking was absolutely swinish: foolscap accounting paper columnised by the age of stock. Each of us could add columns in pounds, shillings and pence by eye, doing the mental arithmetic. You filled in these sheets during the day during stocktaking time, and you did the counting at night at home. They hadn't invented calculators at that time. Mrs Fenwick was my own secretary, and she worked for me for twenty-five years. I could type faster than her with my three fingers, but that wasn't her main function. She was just a terrific woman: she was a great all-round assistant and personality.

We had a lot of office staff, because we had contracting work with journal subscriptions and our academic library supply, rather than public library supply. We did some public library supply, but I never got drawn into the deep-discounting bulk schoolbook supply, because every single one of those companies that did so all went bust. In later years in my life, I always put in a bid for those contracts as what they then called the 'stand-by contractor' – very intelligent of them, because they knew they would go bust. So they had a standby – us – and my terms weren't the same as the guys who were going bust. I wouldn't jeopardise our business or our staff.

We were still the kind of business on George IV Bridge that we had been on the Mound, except we had more space. We had to fill those shelves and sell more stock.

That gradually happened, and the business was very successful. People came to us and we got new customers. There was lots going on and there was interesting publishing at that time. There were some great adventures in publishing from the late 1960s on the national, British, scene. Locally, Edinburgh had Edinburgh University Press under Archie Turnbull, then, which was stunning. I wish I'd kept fifty copies of every book they'd published! Edinburgh University Press was doing brilliant work. Archie Turnbull and George Mackie designed the most beautiful book that had *ever* been made in Edinburgh: Professor Youngson's *The Making of Classical Edinburgh* [1966]. It was lovely to hold, lovely to touch – it felt like a book, and we must have sold *thousands* of them. The photographs were stunning. Well, that was the kind of thing that was going on; there was always something else happening. The trade was active; people were buying books.

Some years after my father's death in 1979, I hooked on a music department to the main shop, and eventually we were the largest purchasers of classical music north of a line from Hull to Leeds, I think. I set it up – I didn't run it – but I had two excellent chaps who did. One of them, Perry Clarke, who died of cancer about three years ago, was with me for about seventeen years. He married Margaret Allan, who must have been with me for some twenty years.

The area became much more of a bookselling locale. There was Grant's remainder bookshop on the corner, by Greyfriars Bobby. That was Ian Grant's cousin, Gordon Grant. He lives still at Currie/Balerno, and he is still a member of the Edinburgh Booksellers' Society. Of course, Ian Grant's antiquarian bookshop was just opposite. Right down at the university just a couple of years later were Jim

Haynes and Andy Muir, who was a pal of mine, and the
Paperback Bookshop. Andy actually worked for Collins,
the publishers. He involved himself in the Paperback
Bookshop and the theatre workshop. The Traverse Theatre
was happening then, founded by Jim and Andy and Nick
Fairbairn. He was a character, too. They were a wonderful
bunch of characters. And the artist, Richard De Marco.
There was a good feeling at the time. That generation
were fairly well educated; people were attuned to buying
books and reading. You could go into those places, and
it didn't matter if you wore a suit or sandals. There was
great jazz going on in Edinburgh as well – lots of music.
Edinburgh was a good place at the time!

William Kay

APPRENTICED IN THE BOOK TRADE

I was born in Galloway. My father was a farmer in a small village called Port William, and I went to the local school, Port William primary school. As I got on I had to go to the high school, which was about seventeen miles away in Newton Stewart, the Douglas Ewart high school. I was there for five years in the Higher grade of the school. I had every intention of going to the university, as I was qualified to do so because of my leaving certificate. But a spanner was thrown in the works in a way: my father was the principal tenant of the late Sir Herbert Mackerill's estate at Monrieff, and as such he was usher at the wedding of one of Sir Herbert's grandson's daughters. The grandson knew my father very well over the years. He had come up to Galloway, as his father had died and he lived with his grandfather, Sir Herbert. And he said to my father at the wedding, 'By the way, what is your young boy William doing?' 'Oh,' he says, 'I think he is going to Glasgow University to study for the ministry. He is so keen on books and is always reading. And he thought he would be suited for the ministry.' Mr Graham said, 'Send him up to the office in Glasgow and we will give him an interview. We could take him on in the book department and give him a training there.' So that is where I landed, a young boy of nearly seventeen, and I went into the book department in Glasgow of John Menzies and Company.

In these days John Menzies was a real power in the book trade in Scotland. I mean it was terrific at wholesale and then eventually retail. But I of course joined the wholesale in Glasgow, which was a branch of the head office in Edinburgh. There were no trade unions in Menzies – it was a non-union house – but they had a training scheme of their own. The young people who met as apprentices in West Nile Street were allocated to departments, for instance, Bibles, fiction and non-fiction. They were first of all taken in to where the book stocks were kept, classified under religion, author – everything went by the alphabet, and you had to be good at the alphabet. You were taught how to receive a book from the publisher, check the invoice and then tick it off. Then you went to the stock room, where all the books were kept under publishers' names alphabetically. Within publishers' sections, everything was kept alphabetically. In fact, knowing the code name of the company was profitable: any prices that were put on books were put in code; a book would be read by the numbers, and it would give you the code and it would give you the name of a book. I can't remember exactly how it worked. We worked in the stock room for about six months, and that was everything except Bibles. They were kept in another part of the building, because they did a terrific business in wholesaling Bibles from Oxford or Cambridge University Press, Eyre and Spottiswoode, and Collins. We had to have a good knowledge of the printed Bible. So that was me in the book department.

Eventually, when I had been there for four years, they said, 'How would you like to take a trip down to Paisley?' – which was only about four miles away – to visit the two

booksellers there, because we sold to these booksellers. So
I went down there and I saw them, and they [head office]
were quite pleased because it just took me a day to go there.
They said, 'Oh well, we are keeping an eye on your progress',
and in a few years' time I was made assistant book manager
of Glasgow, and buyer as well. Glasgow, although it wasn't
the head office, had a very big book department which was
bigger than the head office's book department because of
the population in Glasgow (over a million), compared to
only 400,000 in Edinburgh.

RAILWAY STALLS, BOOKSELLERS AND THE WHOLESALE BUSINESS

Menzies obtained the right to have a bookstall where the
railway said they could in Scotland, and eventually it was
all over Britain. But that was a very small part of the main
book trade, because in Glasgow and Edinburgh, for
instance, we had as our customers the small booksellers
in North Berwick, Aberdeen and Ayr. They would buy
most of their books from John Menzies wholesalers, and
we had book travellers who would go out selling to them,
and in Northern Ireland too. We had very good bookstores
in Coleraine and Londonderry and Belfast, and so on. As
assistant book manager I was in control of buying and
selling the books and the staff. We had a staff of forty-five
in Glasgow at that time.

I used to go twice a year round the country visiting the
main booksellers. Apart from the bigger towns like
Aberdeen, Perth, Glasgow, Edinburgh, Ayr, Dumfries,
there were not many that would have needed calling in.
They did not have the business in a small town like Kelso,
for example. Very often these still bought most of their
books from John Menzies, because they could get them

quickly. If they ordered them from a publisher at that time, the service from London to Scotland was very bad. There was a firm called Billings and Company, but it folded, and there was no real carrier for books only from London. They started to send them by ordinary transport, which was not good at the time. It actually seems to be quite good now. I did go round the booksellers twice a year, because maybe they did have problems with Menzies at the time, or I could help them on in some way. That would be Kirkcaldy, Perth, Inverness and occasionally Stornoway, as they had two good bookshops there, and then down to Dumfries and Galashiels.

When I went down south every year to visit the publishers, I wrote a report every night, and that came to the boardroom in Menzies so that they would know how I was getting on. And when I came back, certain members of the board would ask me about visits I had made and what had happened in more detail. They took an interest. But that was another problem: when I got back at night to my hotel, before I did anything, I had to get a report posted to Edinburgh. They obviously read it all, because when I got back they had queries about certain paragraphs that they wanted to know more about. Generally, if a publisher came to visit Menzies, I would tell the boardroom every morning who was coming. 'Well, would you bring him up to the board-room,' they'd say, and he would go up to see the directors for a chat. I often left them to it for half an hour or so. The publishers, I must say, were very loyal to me.

SETTING UP IN ICELAND
Curiously enough, we set up a very good export business in books with Iceland. It happened because they had the daily papers flown from Glasgow to Reykjavik. We got a

message on the phone from somebody who got the papers saying they were coming into Leith and could I meet them, because they might be prepared to give us their book trade. It was a large book trade, far more than the British shops. There were only two bookshops in Iceland, in Reykjavik, but, by Jove, did they know about books and how to sell them. If they got enquiries for technical books, they passed them to us and we ordered them from the publisher. They also sold a lot of English fiction and non-fiction and travel.

I never was a great drinker, but they could drink me under the table in no time. The first time I went to Iceland, I got in touch with the big wholesaler there, and they said, 'Oh yes, very nice that you are coming to Iceland', and said they would meet me at the airport. It was a funny plane: it came from Copenhagen to Glasgow, so it was often hours late, particularly in the wintertime. It got there about two in the morning, hours late after a bumpy ride, and to my amazement the Icelandic Booksellers' Association, twelve of them, met me at the airport to bid me welcome and take me to my hotel. The job was getting rid of them after they came and saw me settled in my hotel. They had a chat, and I thought, I wonder how to get rid of them. Then I suddenly remembered they would know I got whisky on the plane. So I said, 'If you open that bag, there is a bottle of whisky in it.' And we finished the bottle of whisky, which is the usual way in Iceland.

MENZIES AND BOOK DISCOUNTS
As wholesalers, when we dealt with the publishers we never ordered one book. We were always ordering at least a dozen, and many more, sometimes hundreds or thousands. As wholesalers we could get a discount from the publishers

of 33 per cent – that was the basic discount that went to all booksellers. With paperback orders, they would say, 'Well, if you could order more – you usually order 2,500 but if you ordered 5,000, we will give you an extra discount of 5 per cent over and above the 40 per cent we normally give for paperbacks.' But for other books, of course, it was not anything like as good. So the normal price we got in Menzies from publishers was 33 and another 5 per cent, occasionally 10 per cent or 12 per cent if the numbers were big enough. Our wholesale customers we used to charge 3 pence in the pound. To the proper booksellers, we would only give at the most 33 per cent off, providing we were getting 45 per cent, which happened particularly with paperbacks. But we could not give the retail book-sellers any more than 28 per cent, which was not as good as if they dealt directly with the publishers. However, they had all that trouble of opening an account with the publisher, and the publisher was not all that keen to have them, because they were only small orders to a publisher, single copies at a time.

BUYING FROM D. C. THOMSON

When I was in the book department, I had to go and see the publisher in Dundee, D. C. Thomson. You could not order what you wanted because of a shortage of paper in these days. They would say your allocation for Menzies this year is 10,000, where you could have wanted orders of twelve or thirteen thousand, but the allocation was ten because of shortages. I used to go to Dundee to see them. They were very straightforward to deal with, but I remember being told in Glasgow: 'When you go to visit Thompson in Dundee, make it an appointment to see the retail director, Sidney Moodie. Now when you go to see Mr

Moodie, you do your business and it will all be finished in ten minutes. He will give you a list saying the number of each publication you are going to get in the next year. And after you have had a chat for about ten minutes you ask, would you not like to come to lunch? Whereupon his eyes will light up. You take him to the Royal British Hotel, and you will buy him no more than two large whiskies.' Which he gratefully accepted. He then would ask if you wanted to come and see the directors. 'Yes, certainly.' I met the Thomsons and the Laings. Very nice people, and very interested to know about publishers and how they were doing. I discovered once when they asked me about a publisher that a year later they had obtained a majority share in that company.

MENZIES' QUALITY SERVICE
As far as wholesalers in Scotland, there was only Menzies, apart from one company in Glasgow, William Holmes and Company. There were two Holmes in Glasgow: one was retail and one was wholesale. But they only dealt with the books that were quick sellers, paperbacks really. If someone in Lossiemouth asked for a book, they would tell them to go straight to the publishers. They had no connections with the main book publishers – only Menzies had this. Booksellers used Menzies mainly for the service. Anywhere in Scotland they got a marvellous service, because Menzies had their own transport. If you were a bookseller in Oban and you phoned up for one copy of a book, and we had it in stock, you would get it the next morning. An overnight service all year round, apart from the outer islands, but right up to Inverness and Wick. There was transport going up every day from Edinburgh and Glasgow.

Menzies' old bookshops at the West End (of Glasgow

and Edinburgh) were the foundation of their business. I mean, when Menzies sold the shops, their book business went down – it had to. They had good book departments and well-trained staff. When I was book manager, I used to have a class once a week in the canteen with all the young people who'd joined the company, junior members really, seventeen to about thirty, and we used to go through the elements of buying and stocking books. I thought that, instead of going round the staff individually, I could tell them collectively and get their views on things. Staff had good suggestions, which I sometimes took up. We told them about forthcoming books that might be in demand, so they could keep an eye out for them in their departments. It was always a pleasant meeting every week. They used to ask lots of questions that we were usually able to answer.

On the wholesale side in Edinburgh, we had travellers going round bookshops to solicit business. I was on a visit in Aberdeen, and I was going to Inverness. I stopped off in Huntly to see a bookseller on the way over to Inverness. When I got to Inverness, I discovered I had left my bowler hat behind. I phoned them and they said, 'Yes, Mr Kay, it is here.' I said, 'Just keep it – my bookseller will be up in a month: just give it to him.' And they said, 'Fair enough.' The time went past, and I said to our traveller, 'If you are going that way go and get my bowler from the restaurant, it has the initials W. K.' He came back and phoned me: 'There is no trace of it here.' I said, 'Don't worry. I have another one.' Much later, a year later, he was going up to Wick, and he stopped at a hotel between Inverness and Wick. He saw a bowler hat, and he lifted it off the peg, and it had the initials W. K. He phoned and said, 'I've got your hat, Mr Kay!' It was about 100 miles further north than where I had left it. I don't wear one now. I wore one when I was twenty, but nowadays I never see them, apart from lawyers coming from the court.

WORKING IN EDINBURGH

After spending several years in Glasgow, I was summoned to the head office in Edinburgh and they said, 'We would like you to come as the assistant book manager to the general book manager, Mr Wilson, in Edinburgh, and you will be his official assistant.' That was me in Edinburgh, and I had quite a big job there. My job was to see and know all the publishers in London to buy books. I used to go down to London twice a year for a week, maybe ten days, going round the publishers. Apart from that, they came up to Scotland to visit booksellers. I got to know the publishers well – you had to – and altogether enjoyed the work, but it was very hard going down to London twice a year – the last thing you wanted to do was eat! They all wanted to take you to dinner or lunch, and sometimes when I got back to the hotel at night I refused all offers of dinner and went round to a pub in a back street for a glass of beer and a sandwich. I was fed up of food.

When Mr Wilson retired I became manager. In 1966 I went to London as book manager. After a couple of years there I returned to Edinburgh in 1968, but by then they had they brought in what they called a merchandise manager, who was responsible for buying stationery and toys and writing pads and things, and books. He was a very peculiar man who had only in his life bought boots, not books – some difference. He approached everything from a merchandising point of view: big-picture everything. He knew nothing about books, and he said to me: 'You just look after the books rather than me.' But he kept

sticking his nose in, and eventually was quite objectionable
to me. So I fell out with John Menzies after thirty-odd
years, I think, and left in 1968. But since then Menzies
has been very good, always inviting me to staff functions
to meet people, or to lunch. I have nothing but praise
for them.

BECOMING A BOOKSELLER

I bought a small bookshop in Morningside in Edinburgh,
called Kay's bookshop. I was there for eight years and then
I retired, so that was me out of an active role in the book
trade. It was a suburban bookshop in Morningside, and
we were very lucky. We were on the fringe of where most
of the university professors lived, within a mile, and they
and their wives would come in. It was a very friendly atmosphere, and we had very good customers. We had quite a
lot of connections, but apart from that we had lots of
people coming in from the suburbs and the Southside.
Because there were hardly any parking restrictions at that
time, they would stop on their way and then go on into
Edinburgh to do their general shopping.

Curiously enough for a suburban bookshop, it was the
only good suburban bookshop in Edinburgh. We could not
concentrate on scientific or technical books, but we could
get them. We had a lot of general fiction and good travel
books, a selection of general books and quite a lot of paperbacks. We had a lot of customers who would come in and
say, 'I am looking for a good novel.' Or, 'I am looking for
a nice novel to give.' We always were able to recommend
something that would be acceptable. This was mainly because
I was keen on books and still dealt direct with publishers,
who came from London to see us or sent a rep. There were
reps from London even coming to our shop. Collins,

Nelsons, everybody. We just had about five or six of the big publishers who would come to Edinburgh, but they did not need to come and see us because we did not carry their stuff. They would often come for a drink if they were in town and have a meal with us in our house in Newington.

We also got part of the contract for the public library in Edinburgh, which was a very big part of our business. I mean it was thousands of pounds a year, mainly because I was known in the Booksellers' Association. I was chairman of the Scottish branch before I even went into the shop. I was vice chairman and chairman for a few years, so I knew everybody in the trade and they knew us. I met all the booksellers – the Westlands of Aberdeen, and Glasgow's John Smith & Son. I was very friendly with the managing director there, a Mr John M. Knox. He was a great man, and a great bookseller. I remember when I left for Menzies' head office in Edinburgh, he came up to the office to say goodbye and wish me the best. He said: 'Don't forget when you go to Edinburgh that Glasgow still sells more books than Edinburgh.' In Edinburgh there was Thin's and the Edinburgh Bookshop, Baxendine's and Bauermeister's, who were on the Bridges. Menzies himself said: 'There are three good shops in Edinburgh – Elliot's bookshop, MacNiven & Cameron, and Douglas & Foulis.' Menzies bought them all, but I would not say they prospered as booksellers under Menzies. We knew the Hogbens of the Edinburgh Bookshop very well, the family who owned it. There were no other suburban bookshops. There did not seem the need for them, but then they had the good bookshops in the city centre. Glasgow had good bookshops in the centre, but only two or three.

James Glover

STARTING IN THIN'S

I was non-traditional. I left school, joined the RAF, and started the job in Thin's when I left in 1946. There was a great camaraderie among the staff. They were a very good crowd. There were about four or five people in the back shop, employed to pack up parcels. It was run by a very elderly man. His assistant was a chap called Jimmy Burnett, who then took on the running of that department. He ran it for years and years and years, long after I was away, in fact. Jimmy Burnett had a great team of workers. Thin's had the stationery department on the corner of the South Bridge shop. Well, that wasn't Thin's to begin with; that was a fur shop in the old days. The furriers were broken into on one memorable occasion. The thieves didn't actually come in via the fur shop: they went down below to the Thin's basement, and they came along and burrowed up the floorboards into the furrier's. But Thin's some years later bought that fur shop and changed it all over.

HAMISH HAMILTON

In 1959 I went to Hamish Hamilton as a sales rep. At that time I was living down in East Lothian, in Dunbar, and I travelled back and forward every day. I went all over the country, really. I had a set salary and I was also paid commission on sales. They eventually stopped that: they thought I was earning too much money because I was going to the biggest library suppliers. Hamilton had a pretty strong literary list, though not compared to the Hutchisons, Collins and Heinemann. A big list, but it was a strong literary list, a good list, and it suited me down to the ground. I covered the whole of Scotland, Ireland and the north of England, which was a big territory. But I was not like the Collins rep: I did not have to call on every bookseller. The Collins rep did have calls in the Western Isles, but this did not apply to us. So I covered a big geographical area and also carried Phaidon Press, the art publishers, who at the time were privately owned by Bela Horowitz. His daughter married a fellow called Dr Miller, and he was the managing director. It was an interesting time.

I would try to do Edinburgh and Glasgow in a six-week cycle. North of Scotland and Aberdeen I would maybe go four times a year, or something like that. Ireland I went to three times a year, to Dublin and Belfast, and three times a year to the Irish provinces. It took in places like Limerick and Cork. I did not do that in the winter months, but I covered that twice a year. I visited all the shops I could, unless they were small, specialist shops sell-ing only motorcycle books, or something. My biggest turnover came from the north-west of England by far, because that was where all the big library suppliers were. Holt Jackson, that was very big business, because they bought hundreds and hundreds of copies, both fiction and non-fiction, mainly in sheets, and then rebound them themselves. When you are talking about fiction, you are talking about libraries, because what the libraries take makes a huge difference to your initial print run and what you sell. Later on, if it takes off in the country, then the figures go through the roof.

I remember saying to my wife Molly, when I had been on the road six or seven years, 'I do enjoy this, but I do not plan to do this until I am fifty.' A year later I went to London. I had a phone call from Jamie Hamilton to ask whether I would like to go and talk to the board, and they appointed me as sales manager in 1965 or 1966, and that was it. I did that until 1973. I went on the board in 1968 or 1969. I enjoyed that fully. As sales manager I had complete responsibility for all the sales and marketing, including all the sales promotion and PR. The PR was run at that time by a man called Leo Cooper, who was married to Jilly Cooper, the author. Leo was only there for eighteen months, and then there was a succession of other people. You had responsibility for running the reps – there were about seven of them. There were visits abroad to make. I used to go to Paris, Amsterdam, Brussels, the Hague about three time a year. I also went to Canada, Australia and New Zealand. These were general trips to see if we could improve our sales in these areas, and to give a briefing to the reps on the job.

We were not big enough to have our own overseas reps, so in Canada we were represented by Nelsons in Toronto. I went out there and briefed their reps about what we expected. We were competing for their time as these reps were carrying about four lists. We were represented by Hutchinsons in the early days in Australia, and Hodder in New Zealand. Of course, there was managing all the office staff and the warehouse, which involved me in matters that I had never come across in my life, like the SOGAT union, because in the warehouse there were about twenty-seven union men. We had a great deal of trouble with the unions – the personality disputes were endless.

AN HONEST TRADE

There was a fellow called Ogsten, who was assistant trade manager at Nelsons. He became a rep with Collins in the north of England, and then the Collins sales manager in London. He and I were asked by a lady called Mary Perry, who was the Publishers' Association training officer, to give a class about three times a year at St Hilda's College in Oxford University to students who wanted to learn about publishing. It was a course for editorial people, and this class was for sales people. It was a double turn, and we did that for some years. One other thing I did – I was actually a director of four or five businesses at one time, because we were all involved in Hamish Hamilton, it being such a small set-up. Elmtree Books we started as an offshoot, doing cookery books and that sort of thing. Then there was Hamish Hamilton books and Hamish Hamilton Children's and, of course, Phaidon Press.

POPULAR SELLERS OF THE TIME

Over the whole period I was at Hamish Hamilton, some of our big sellers were *Catcher in the Rye* by J. D. Salinger, novels by Susan Hill and Nancy Mitford, and books of that class and quality. In Ireland, of course, the Irish authors always went well. Hamilton published stories of Frank O'Connor. Later [1970] we did the *Life of Brendan Behan* by Ulick O'Connor. That was good, because we had a party in Dublin that was something to remember – or something to forget, I would say. Dominic Behan, who was Brendan's brother, was an absolute hoot at the party. Jennifer Johnson was a good Irish author.

Publishers like Hamilton published a lot of things that were bestsellers, but also a lot that were not. I remember one comment after we published J. K. Galbraith's great sellers *The Affluent Society* [1958] and *The Great Crash*

[1955]. He wrote a book called *Made to Last* [1964], which was about his Scottish predecessors who had gone to Canada to live, and only a few people bought it. He went on and wrote a book about when he was American ambassador to India that not many people wanted to read [*Ambassador's Journal: A Personal Account of the Kennedy Years*, 1969]. We were having a discussion in the office one day and somebody said, 'Do you think we should publish it?' And I said, 'There is no doubt it is J. K. Galbraith, but the sales are not there. They are going down. We should think about what we are going to give him as a royalty at this time.' Somebody said to the chairman, 'Think about the prestige', and he said, 'We are lousy with prestige.' Which I thought was quite good. Because although our list was not as big as Cape, it was that type, quite good, and it would be a pity for that list to disappear.

One book I said I didn't think would sell. I am not particularly proud of that. Roger Machell brought us a book, which was a Gothic novel by Susan Howatch called *Penmarric* [published by Hamish Hamilton in 1971]. She is a lovely girl, and when it is not the type of book you read yourself, you have to be careful. I said, 'I do not see this, Roger', and he said, 'This is a bestseller.' Anyway, he was completely right and I was completely wrong. I think every publisher in London turned down *Watership Down*; it came to Hamilton before my time, but I am not saying I would have spotted it. The Tolkien books, too. I would not be too good at judging them. But I had a certain input. I would very often get the proof from the editor asking me, 'If you can read this by Friday, let us know what you think.' I liked that side of it. I loved what I did; with a full education, I would have ideally worked on the editorial side.

I think that bestsellers sell well everywhere. This is one of the things that Hamilton was good at. Jamie Hamilton was a man of great flair and charm. His great forte, apart from the fact that he owned the company, was that he had this rapport with people. He could charm the birds off the trees, and he would get these American authors like Robert Ruark and Truman Capote. He was not an easy person to get on with; latterly not that well. But people like Hamilton could get these authors despite the fact, I suspect, that the sales force at Hamilton struggled against the larger firms. We had something like five reps covering the whole of the UK and Ireland and the continent, whereas some of our colleagues probably had five in Scotland and twenty-five in other areas.

Jamie Hamilton, the chairman, used to come up from London occasionally and we would have lunches. The first lunch he came to, after I became the representative in this part of the world, would have been 1961. Later, we had dinner in the George, and I took him and his wife, who was an Italian countess, back to Turnhouse airport. The plane was delayed, so he suggested that he go and visit Compton Mackenzie. Well, this was fine, and I drove him along, and they insisted that I go in. I didn't think they would. Mackenzie was an old boy by then, and he sat with a rug around him and told one story after another. They were friends, of course, which was a highlight. I had a little contact with authors then, but very much more later when I went to London and became sales rep and then sales director.

RUNNING A BOOKSHOP
A colleague of mine, Michael Pooley – he was actually my assistant – had some money and bought a bookshop. He asked if I would run it and would have a small share in the

business with a view to expanding it. I thought about it, and eventually I said 'yes'. I went to Marlborough and the White Horse bookshop in 1973. Marlborough was a very pleasant place to be, and we got very involved in the town and the chamber of commerce. We were based in Marlborough the whole time, even though we had shops in Newbury, some just outside Swindon, and the Bell bookshop in Henley-on-Thames. Then my partner, Michael Pooley, who owned the business, gave up work in Hamish Hamilton and took over the Newbury shop. When I was in Thin's I was running a department, concentrating on that department; whereas at Marlborough I was involved in all of the business, especially in the early days when we bought the Henley bookshop. I spent a lot of time running back and forwards until we appointed someone to it. I got a letter from Margaret, who was running *The Times* bookshop in London, saying that, 'I see you have got involved with buying the Henley Bookshop and said I would be interested if you would consider me.' Well, she took the job and she is still there.

We had quite a few signings in Marlborough because, as well as having signings in the shop, Marlborough council ran a bi-monthly antiques fair in the town hall and we used to get an offer to come with people like Roald Dahl and P. D. James and people like that to do signings. It was a great success, and people were desperate to come on. Laurie Lee and Dick Francis would come back from Florida once a year and would always do a signing at Newbury. One of the most successful signings I had was back at Hamish Hamilton with someone with whom I got very friendly for several years, David Niven. We published a book by him called *The Moon's a Balloon* [1972], which had an enormous sale, and taking him round London for this was great fun.

When the staff at Marlborough got to a certain size, we had to change the building with the fire doors and things like that. Then we got the Marlborough College business. The bookshop had not had the college business until we got there. It put us on the map. As a general shop we had large premises, with a lovely old building stretching miles back. So we had art materials and a big art department, and a lovely room upstairs that overlooked Marlborough high street and was the children's department, which was good when we had authors to visit. Vera Horner, who ran the children's department, was the first bookseller ever to get Dick King-Smith to come and do a book signing and talk to the children.

Marlborough is a historic area with the connection with Cromwell and the Savernake Forest. The local books were exceptionally good. This was where my partner was especially good in the Newbury shop, because he knew all about horse racing. This was a great area for horse racing, and the Dick Francis signings were a huge success. People would come down from London – all the jockeys like Johnny Francome and Bob Champion, whose horse won the National. Newbury was great for that. Henley was a great general bookshop, with literary novels and biographies, and at Marlborough we did all that and academic and art books. It was a very good area, as there is a lot of cash in the Henley-on-Thames and Marlow area.

One of the things at Marlborough was that I was able to tie up my customers with books that they would want. Lady Devlin and Lord Devlin used to come in, and he loved, just devoured, the Brother Cadfael series I put him on to. I felt I could do that. I could read the novels, and people would come in and I would say, 'Have you tried that?' If they liked it, whenever a new one came out by that author you would say, 'You know there is a new so-and-so.' Another one of my good customers was Norman Foster the architect, now Lord Foster. He would come in every Saturday and I would guide him towards a book. He hardly ever did not take it. I had a good idea about what different types of book would suit different people.

We did a lot of local advertising in the local press, especially at Christmastime, and also with the signings. We did two other things: we advertised regularly in a racing paper; and the other thing we did, which was due to Michael, is that we advertised in the diplomatic corps. There was a paper for diplomat corps wives, and we advertised there. We would send any book to any British embassy in the world. There were often big parcels going from this British bookshop in Charles Street to the embassies. But that was specialised trade.

When we first went to Marlborough, Michael went round wholesalers before coming into the shop. He used to go round the publishers on a Monday, pick the books up in the car and bring them down to us – which was a great boon. In those days, a few people did it; in the old days the booksellers had collectors. Thin's had a lady who used to go round all the publishers in Edinburgh, and in London they had collectors who would go round all the warehouses. We picked up on a Monday and delivered on a Tuesday. It worked out that Michael could do it, as he then lived in London. He later moved out to Newbury, but then he still did it. The biggest changes later came in ordering – the introduction of tele-ordering in particular was a huge change. I would think that tele-ordering came in with us in about 1980, because we were quite a bit behind the big booksellers.The business was to convince the girls that we could type the orders in the evening and, if someone would remember to switch the telephone over, then the orders would be away the next morning. Of course, there were teething problems. It did not work very well at the start, but I am sure that it works like clockwork now. We were told of all these innovations at the booksellers' conference. I found that the booksellers' conference latterly was the 'same-old, same-old', but you did meet all the publishers there. You could make your points and talk to them about things that were coming out. That meant you could get early advance, advertise what was coming out, and put your Christmas catalogue out early. We had a Christmas catalogue for years.

LUCKY CAREER
I retired in 1988. I was very lucky the way things fell into place. Each move came at the right time. I was lucky, because had I gone to any other publisher, I would never have enjoyed it as much as Hamish Hamilton, with the type of books that they were publishing, and the Phaidon Press, of course. It all worked out well.

Robert Henderson

EARLY CAREER

My primary school was Lochend, and my secondary school
was Leith Academy. Mind you, I was only there for two
and a half years, as in those days you could leave at
fourteen. That is what I did because my father was away
during the war. It was 1942: he had always been in the Post
Office telephones, my elder brother had been in the
Post Office telephones, and it was assumed that I would
be. However, they would not take you at the Post Office
at fourteen and a half straight from school, as they felt
that this was spoiling your education. On the other hand,
they would take you if you had left school and had had
another job. So I went to Tomlin Brothers, seed merchants
in Leith, as an office boy for a month or two just to get
an interview with the GPO. But the Post Office rejected
me because of my eyesight. I can only see with one eye –
the other one is pretty useless, always has been – and they
wouldn't take me. So I then went to J. B. MacKenzie, on
Saughton Hill, as an apprentice electrician. I was there
for about three and a half years, until I was eighteen. Just
before I was eighteen, I got a letter from the king asking
me to go and shoot Germans, so I reluctantly went into
the army. The army occasionally does things right, and I
ended up as a electrician in the Royal Mechanical

Engineers and I was there for three years, latterly as an instructor. I picked up tuberculosis in Germany immediately after the war, and I was discharged and told to get a light job. I then went to a rehabilitation unit at Granton and the guy that was in charge of that was a friend of Jack Hogben, who had the Edinburgh Bookshop, William Brown Bookseller, at 57 George Street. He was looking for somebody who could read. Though I could read, I wasn't a literary character by any means. So I went there and did everything from sweeping floors to serving customers, packing parcels – anything and everything. I was there for many years and I gradually became the buyer, technically the manager, although Jack Hogben, who was the managing director, was still there.

THE EDINBURGH BOOKSHOP
The company at that time was owned by Will Y. Darling, who had been Lord Provost among other things and of course owned Darling's on Princes Street and Robert Grant and Sons, which was attached to Darling's and had a communicating door through to it. Grant's moved up to George Street and didn't do well at all, as it relied on passing trade, whereas William Brown had everybody who was anybody as their customer: everybody from the Duke of Argyll to Lord James Douglas Hamilton as their customers. Lord James used to come in as a schoolboy and ask me if he could look at the books. It was that sort of place. It was the upmarket bookshop. Then Darling decided in the 1950s that the two shops should amalgamate, because William Brown had a big basement that was just a midden. So Robert Grant came and joined us. It sold a lot of stationery goods. Willie Darling became the chief shareholder of the whole bang shoot. The stationery

department of Grant's expanded and went into the basement, which was dug down three feet deeper than it had been. There had been only six-foot-six of headroom – you could walk about, but it was not high enough to let the public go in. It was quite interesting, as when they started to dig down they discovered that the house had been one of the first houses on George Street to be built. It had no foundations. It was just built on the clay and that was it. It was boulders that it was built on, and they had to underpin the whole thing to keep the thing up.

The amalgamation worked fine, but the telephone operator used to say 'Good morning. William Brown, booksellers. Robert Grant and Sons.' I said at one of the regular meetings: 'This is awful cumbersome. Can we not just call it one thing? Can we not call it the Edinburgh Bookshop?' So that is what we did. I always remember Ainslie Thin saying: 'Robert, you are not the Edinburgh Bookshop. You are *an* Edinburgh Bookshop.' I responded: 'No. We are *the* Edinburgh Bookshop.' All the booksellers in Edinburgh got on well; we helped each other a great deal.

When it was William Brown, there was only really about five of us; Mrs Lyle was the only woman. We had no girls. We had an office upstairs, and they provided a girl down for the cash desk. In these days there was a cash desk that was all glass, with a hole for the money to go out and in. Jack Ross was the manager when I went there. Michael Hogben, Jack Hogben's son, was supposed to be working there, but he did not do an awful lot. Michael was a character and we got on very well, but he was not one of life's workers, and he got away with murder. They lived up the stairs in the top flat, and Mrs Hogben was a poor wee soul. She was a nervous wreck, and she thought that she had every disease under the sun. She read the medical books and thought she had everything. She definitely was not well; she was ill, but . . . Bill Parry on the staff was a character. He should have been an actor; he was a nutcase, but an awful nice bloke.

Jim Abbey was the antiquarian bookseller. We had quite a large antiquarian section. He was a really nice man, and he had been there with William Brown as an apprentice well before the First World War because he got the Military Medal in the First World War. He was fifty-seven years with William Brown Bookseller Limited, man and boy. I remember saying to him one day that we had put a wee plaque at the front of the shop to commemorate it. 'Really,' he said, 'You haven't asked me.' I said: 'Come out and look – fifty-seven years.' Of course, we went out and saw the number 57 on the shop, number 57 George Street. He didn't drive, and I would drive him round the big houses. At that time there were a lot of libraries in houses selling up, be it for death duties or getting rid of them for money. I used to go with him, and my knowledge of antiquarian books was very limited, always was. But he would start at one side of the library and I would start at another, and I would pull things out that I thought he might be interested in. I knew what was *not* of interest to him, but that was about all. We used to go to the sale, where they were up to all tricks. They all watched Jim, because he was the knowledgeable man. So if I pointed something out, he would say: 'Robert, shove it to the back. Put other books on top of it.' We did this in the hope that the other booksellers would not notice it, because the items would be sold in lots – bookcase by bookcase. He would sometimes give me a catalogue that he would mark up in his alphabetical code of the prices that he was prepared to bid to. The thing was that he would go in and sit at the front, and then I would go and sit up at the back. Jim would bid for a lot up to a certain sum and then stop. Everybody else would think it was not worth any more. Then this voice from the back would bid. If he'd gone for it, they would all want it, but if he lost interest that implied it was not worth any more than that and they would lose interest too. This was just sharp practice on our part.

William Brown originally had been an antiquarian book-shop and was situated on the other side of George Street in a building that was owned by the Millers, probably number 20 or something like that. I believe it was in 1947, before my time, that it moved to 57 George Street and opened a general shop when Jack Hogben came out of the air force. He had been a fighter pilot in the First World War and then he was in the Second World War as an intelligence officer. He was the chap who interviewed Hess when Hess came to Scotland and was brought to the RAF. Hogben was the first senior person to interview him. He was a very correct person, but very abrupt. He had a thing about people getting time off; he hated anybody to get time off. If somebody said: 'My granny has died – I have to go to the funeral', he'd reply: 'When is the funeral? Half-past two. Well, you could be back here by three.' It was very much that sort of thing. He retired eventually, and I took over. He died on the sixtieth anniversary of the Royal Air Force at a reception at Holyrood. He dropped down dead. And the devil had his funeral on a holiday Monday, so the staff didn't need to get time off to go!

(Lord James Douglas Hamilton wrote a book about Hess called *Motive for a Mission* [1971]. That is interesting because he came to me with a typed galley proof and asked me if I thought it was worth publishing. I read it and said I thought it was most interesting, fascinating. 'Who would publish it?' I said I thought it was the type of book Macmillan would do. 'I will send it to Uncle Harold.' I knew Harold Macmillan well but I would certainly never call him Uncle Harold, but he obviously did.)

Will Y. Darling died in 1962. He was an awful character. He always wore a diamond stud in his cravat – it was not a tie. He always wore his top hat and a silver mantled cane and he walked along Princes Street like he owned Edinburgh – though he nearly did. He always called me Charles, and Lady Darling would say: 'It is not Charles. It is Robert.' 'Yes, yes.' Then going out the door he would say, 'Goodbye, Charles.' He never learnt that my name was not Charles. When Darling died, Sir John Imrie, who was a friend of his, bought the shares and the business continued under his direction; not that he interfered much. Campbell White was his man on the spot. He was a director of Henderson and Bisset up on Causewayside. Campbell used to come in on a Saturday morning, and he would always say, 'Everything all right, Robert?' I would always say 'yes' – even if the place had burned down, I would have said 'yes'. I never told Campbell anything, certainly not anything bad. We got on fine without him. He was a nice guy; he was quite harmless, but I never told him anything unless I had to.

EDINBURGH BOOKSELLERS

There were characters in the book trade when I started. The manager of Robert Grant and Sons before they joined up with us was John Young, who smoked a pipe. He did not smoke tobacco in it; he smoked matches. He lit his pipe every ten seconds, and you could follow him round the shop and there would be a trail of broken matches. The bookseller was Harold Forrester. He was the brother of Fordie Forrester, who bought H. T. McPherson in Dunfermline; Bill Forrester, the son of Fordie, took over the business and I knew him well. Harold was in Robert Grant and Sons and he never wrote anything down. I worked there for a brief period – they were terribly short staffed and I had gone along to help. Harold had one eye which looked that way and one that looked the other; he used to shout 'Boy', and I never knew if it was me he wanted or not. He used to say: 'If I am not looking at you, you are the one I want.' But he never wrote anything down and he remembered everything. He had a small desk and a stool, and at the end of the day he would smoke in the corner. He would say 'Lady Johnson got this', and he would charge it to the account, and 'somebody else wanted this'. But of course he forgot things. Lady Johnson came in for her book. 'Oh yes, I have it, and what was the book again?' and he would come through the back to me and say, 'Run along to Douglas & Foulis and see if they have a copy.'

One thing happened there that I thought was absolutely hilarious. There was a wee girl that came into the shop, and she was the daughter of Sheriff Harold Leslie QC. She came in to buy a book. She had five shillings, and the book was seven and sixpence. Bold Harold said: 'Don't worry! I will put it on a horse in the 3.30. You come back when you have finished school, and you will get your book and you will get your winnings because it is a sure-fire winner.' And of course the damn horse did win! The girl came back and got her change and the book and she was delighted. She went home and told her mother, and her mother was horrified. They came in on Saturday morning and kicked up hell. The father didn't, as he was an awfully nice man, but the mother kicked up about encouraging her daughter. I don't know what would have happened if the horse had lost. I am sure he would have just given her the book, and he might even have put his hand in his pocket. I got on very well with him, but he was a case. His brother Fordie was very different in appearance and behaviour. He ran everywhere; he would burst in the door at 100 miles an hour.

We used to collect books – we had a boy who did it. I used to do it for some time on a motorbike. All the orders that you got that day, you would write up in a book and go round the other shops and see if you could get copies. We all gave each other copies. We did not hold back. We just kept a record of the amount of money. Once a year we would meet and square up between the booksellers. Sandy Douglas ran Douglas & Foulis. Another bookseller left Douglas & Foulis when they became part of the Menzies group and he opened a shop in the Grassmarket with books and gifts. McNiven & Wallace was on the west end of Princes Street, and Elliot's was on the east end. That had originally been owned by Andrew Elliot, who was a publisher; he became the Moray Press along with old Mr Fisher. Elliot's became part of the Menzies shop on the east end, beside Woolworths. Vic Beveridge was the manager there. We all helped each other at that time. Later on, in the early 1950s, this system broke down a bit. There weren't so many booksellers in Edinburgh – many such as Elliot's and Douglas & Foulis had been taken over by Menzies – and we were not so pally, if you like.

Bill Bauermeister and I always kept up our cooperation. At about five o'clock at night we would phone each other and list any orders we had taken. If he had them, he would pass them down as required and we would deliver them. If I phoned Bauermeister's, the voice would come on the phone. Both father and son would sound the same, and I would say: 'Is that you or your father?' Bill senior would always say, 'I had a father too, you know!' We got on very well and really helped one another without any feeling of competition. If there were any foreign books ordered, we would always request them from Bauermeister's. Bill senior was full of fun, and I always remember he came to a Booksellers' Association dinner wearing an Iron Cross. His father, Bill junior's grandfather, was German – whether he had got it in the First World War, I don't know. [See the Bill Bauermeister interview in this volume.] Everybody thought this was hilarious. 'Oh, that is why Germany lost the war.' It was a nice atmosphere.

We also met socially. There was a group called the Bookmen that was formed in the early 1950s. Graham Fraser, who was William Collins representative, was a big man in the book trade – a big fellow, six foot tall. He started the Scottish Bookmen, and we would have an annual dinner alternating in Glasgow or Edinburgh and a dance. This was really for the publishers' reps and the booksellers, people who met regularly in business. The 'high heid yins' didn't tend to come. I don't even think they were members. It was the people that we knew – we were not in touch with the chairmen – it was the sales managers that we knew.

Every year there was a Booksellers' Association conference, and we went to most of them. I was for a time secretary of the Booksellers' Association. The Scottish branch met three times a year and I took the minutes. The secretary and the chairman were on the council of the Booksellers' Association in London, and I had to go down to a meeting every month in London in Buckingham Palace Road. It was Book Tokens Limited who owned the building. Book tokens were great: it was money for old rope – you were selling bits of card. The booksellers bought these stamps at a discount of 12.5 per cent. The chap who sold the book took the token in exchange and got the value of the token less 12.5 per cent, so Book Tokens Ltd made in theory nothing out of it except they sold the cards at five pence or ten pence. In fact, they made an awful lot of money, as many book tokens were never exchanged or were lost or shoved in drawers and forgotten. The Booksellers' Association was subsidised dramatically by Book Tokens Limited, as they had hundreds of pounds. They owned the building in Buckingham Palace Road and charged a nominal rent to the Booksellers' Association. Apparently when they first thought up the idea, they asked the Publishers' Association to go in, but they said it would never work, so the BA went ahead alone. Of course, the Publishers' Association was kicking itself. These book tokens could be cashed anywhere that was a member of the Booksellers' Association. This was a strict condition: to deal in book tokens you had to be a member of the Booksellers' Association. The BA subscription was dependent on your turnover: if you made so much, you paid so much. There was a maximum subscription of £250 a year, which rang a bell for the really big boys. It meant that the Booksellers' Association was stronger because of this.

At that time in Edinburgh there was also the George Street bookshop owned by Peter Cummings. He again in the early 1950s said he was going to be retiring; he offered me a job and said I would have the business. But I did not like the man very much – he was an oddball. Then across the road from us in the Edinburgh Bookshop there was Bruntons. John Pearson owned that. He wasn't a member of the Booksellers' Association, but he would take book tokens and spend them in our shop and we would give him a discount.

LEAVING THE EDINBURGH BOOKSHOP

I left because of money. At that time Jack Hogben was still managing director. He came in in the morning and read the mail – he read everything, including all the publishers' circulars. He sat there until half past ten, and he would then come down and read me the letters. 'Lady Gainford wants a copy of . . .' I used to take the letters and say, 'I can read – just leave me.' I then carried out all the instructions in the letters. He would go up with his pal, a chap called Morland, who was the company lawyer. He, too, came in every morning, and the pair of them went up at about 11 a.m. and sat in the coffee room until 1 p.m. Hogben then came down and went through the orders with a chap called Jimmy Glover, who was the Menzies rep. [See the James Glover interview in this volume.] Menzies was trying to get into the wholesale book market at that time, which was very difficult. Simpkin Marshall had tried this earlier with Ken Harrison, who had been Menzies rep. He went to Simpkin Marshall, and he opened a shop round on Rose Street Lane as a small warehouse. But it did not work, as booksellers always loathed using wholesalers because of the reduced terms. We received 25 per cent discount, whereas when we went to the publishers directly we got 33.3 per cent. We never actually discounted anything to one another. We always just kept the balance, and if one account with another bookseller got out of hand, then the other one would just come down to the shop and pick out some Chambers' dictionaries or something that he could sell to make it up.

We just dealt with the stock between one another; it was purely a barter arrangement. I was paid sweeties to do all the work. I had a couple of children and I was offered more money to leave for a job at Nelson's.

GAMEKEEPER TURNED POACHER

I was offered the post of representative for Scotland of Thomas Nelson's in 1962. I went as the rep there, and I wasn't there any length of time when Ronnie Nelson, who owned Nelson's, latched on to me. He was a railway fanatic; he knew the time of any train. He had a flat in the West End, in Ainslie Place or Moray Place, and he used to phone me at home and ask me: 'Robert, would you run me down to Peebles in the morning?' 'I have appointments,' I replied – I was working as his company's rep; 'Oh, just cancel them.' He treated me like his chauffeur. It did not do my commission any good at all, I can tell you. I ran him to the Cross Keys Hotel in Peebles to meet people from Michael Joseph. They also owned the Good Housekeeping imprint that did all the cookery books. They in effect bought into Nelson's. I ran him to a meeting to discuss this. I had to lose myself for a couple of hours. No way did I know what was going on. From a personal point of view I discovered that I was not only working for Nelson's but also Michael Joseph and a whole lot of American publishers that I had not heard of. From then on, we did not get on very well. I did not get on with Dick Douglas Boyd. At meetings in London, they would all discuss something and then Dick would say, 'What does our Scottish friend say?' And I would say, 'Bollocks!' – because it was. We did not really get on.

I was really just a salesman to them. When I first represented Nelson's, I would try to sell as many books

as I could to booksellers. They were mostly my friends, and
I had some discretion in making terms. I could give them
better terms; I had a little power – not much, but a little.
But with the new group I became just a salesman. The idea
was to sell as many books as possible. I remember Michael
Joseph published a beautiful book on Tutenkhamun. I was
given quotas: I was told I had to sell 200 to Thin's and
100 to the Edinburgh Bookshop; 2,000 to John Menzies.
I went to see one or two booksellers, and I never mentioned
numbers but tried to sell as many as I could. I always tried
to bear in mind what kind of shop it was and the fact that
some shops could not sell things other shops could – that
a shop around the corner can sell stuff that they never
could. There is no point loading people up with hundreds
of copies when they can only sell a dozen, as it creates
bad feeling. In the old days, when I was a bookseller, most
of the publishers that came to see me trusted me. They
were my friends, and while there was the odd chancer
among them, most of them would not oversell something
as they knew damn well that it would not work. Dick
phoned me up and said he was not happy with the figures
of the Tutenkhamun book. He was coming up to Glasgow
and he would like to meet me in Holmes MacDougall,
which was mainly a library supplier at that time, though
it owned bookshops as well. Jimmy Suttie was the buyer
there. He had been a welder in Dundee in the shipyards,
and he called a spade a shovel. He was an awfully nice
guy and a very clever fellow. Jimmy knew his business. I
met Dick in Holmes. I had sold them 300 copies earlier.
Dick came in and Jimmy asked, 'Who is this?' I introduced
him. 'Oh, aye. What are you here for?' Dick said, 'I am
here to increase the subscription to Tutenkhamun. You
have ordered only 300 copies', and Jimmy said to me, 'My

God. You must have bought me a good lunch that day.'
(I probably had.) Dick then said: 'Oh, Mr Suttie, with a
business like this you should be having 1,000 at least.'
Jimmy stood up and said: 'Put your arse down here on
my chair. If you are going to run my business, you better
sit in my chair.' That was the end of that.

BACK TO BOOKSELLING

I was only there a couple of years between 1962 and 1964,
as it was not the job it was meant to be. The Americans
produced a revised standard version of the Bible, and
Nelson's bought the publishing rights to it. It was all being
handled in London. I went down to a meeting, ostensibly
to describe what kind of binding we wanted. I said: 'What
we want is a plain black Bible – no cross.' They had all
been done, and they all had crosses on them. I said: 'What
the hell am I here for, then?' I told the people in London
that if the Bibles had a cross on them, we were not going
to sell them to the Free Church, to which this was Popery.
The Free Kirk was very strict; the Bible had to be plain
and black. I remember another time getting a phone call
from the bookseller in Stornoway to say he had never seen
me. I told my superiors: 'Okay. I will cancel all my meetings
for next week.' 'What do you mean?' 'I am going to
Stornoway – do you know where it is? It will take me a
day to drive there, another day on the ferry.' 'Oh. Is it an
island?' They had not got a clue. They thought Scotland
was a county like Kent that you could do in a day – nip
up to Inverness and back. I was in the Edinburgh Bookshop
as a rep one day, and Sir John Imrie was in the shop. The
conversation went: 'Do you miss it?' 'Yes!' 'Would you like
to come back? You come back and he [Hogben] will retire
in three months' time.' So I did that. I went back to the

Edinburgh Bookshop from 1964 to 1975. I was the manager, although I only looked after the books – there was a chap, Russell, who looked after the stationery.

I was offered a new job in 1975 in the Grand Hotel in Bristol at three in the morning. I was approached in the gentlemen's convenience, I may say – 'Did I want a job?' This was to run the book side of Grant Educational in Union Street in Glasgow. It was mainly textbooks for schools, but there was also a paperback shop, and a general shop in Hardwick Street. They had a few branches. I met the people from Wyndham's, who were the theatrical people – they owned most of the theatres in the country. There were two Americans who ran the business, whose names I will not mention, because in my opinion they were crooks. I was offered shares that were standing at 40p., and I was offered an option of 20,000 shares at 20p. I didn't take them up, I am glad to say, as after that they went down to 1p. They did a Maxwell on the business and took money left, right and centre out of it. This was some time after I went to join them. We initially opened a shop in Stirling, and things were going well. We had the shop in Union Street and bought the shop next door and made that a purely paperback shop. I was retail director for all of these.

We had a contract for the supply of schools' textbooks. We had a warehouse and three or four vans and sent textbooks to the schools, paid through the local authority. Any money from individual schools went through the shops, but this was separate from the local authority contract. Anyway, we had more money taken out of the business than should have been taken out. It got to the stage when I could not pay publishers' bills. I had to try to speak to friends in London and ask for more time – it

was not a pleasant time at all. The crux came when the two
gentlemen phoned from London and asked if I could go
round to the Crédit Lyonnais in Glasgow and see the
manager. I was to pick up a chequebook and confirm an
overdraft of £250,000. I said: 'We don't need an overdraft.
We already have a huge overdraft at the Royal Bank. We
need another overdraft like a hole in the head.' 'Oh, no!
Do this!' So I saw the French banker. I thought I would
pay some of the accounts that I was concerned about –
Collins, Heinemann, the big boys. I no sooner sat down to
do this than I got a call to say: 'Robert, there is a crisis here.
Could you write a cheque for £250,000 to Joseph Bloggs,
Esquire', or somebody. I said no, and we had a blazing row
on the phone. They ended up coming up and I told them
where to stick their job. 'You can't leave on a contract.' I
said the contract had expired a few months back, as I had
been there six years, and 'Good afternoon! I am off.' I
actually had a visit from the fraud squad afterwards and I
told them what I knew. The firm went into liquidation, but
I did not want to get involved. Before I resigned, I could
see myself up in front of the sheriff, who was asking: 'Where
has all the money gone?' I did not know. I know that they
borrowed a lot to give to W. H. Allan, because it was toiling.
And then W. H. Allan was sold to Heinemann; it was in the
Bookseller that they got £1.1 million. I phoned the managing
director and asked for the money they owed us, but he
knew nothing about it. So that was the bad period.

AUTHORS

On the other hand, we did meet an awful lot of interesting
people. I used to say I had had lunch with Anthony Eden
and dinner with Winston Churchill. Any author who was
anyone was brought up to Scotland in the 1960s and 1970s

by the publishers. The nicest person was Sir Alec Douglas-Home. He used to come in a lot to the Edinburgh Bookshop, and he was an awful nice guy, a real charmer. Churchill I think I exchanged six words with – there was a clique of hangers-on with Churchill and the publishers. I was an 'also-ran' then. There would maybe be a dozen of us at the George Hotel from Thin's, Menzies, Elliot's, and the Edinburgh. We met a lot of authors like David Niven, who was a character. I always remember we had a dinner for him up in Prestonfield. He was staying at the Caledonian, or somewhere like that. I was chatting to him and he said he had had an experience in the Cally. He had gone into the lift, and an American elderly lady with blue hair had come in and kept looking at him. Eventually she said, 'Pardon me. Did you use to be David Niven?' He was a case, absolutely. We had a fair number of signing sessions latterly. One wee incident was that Douglas Patterson, who was Faber's rep, came to me and said could I have a signing session for this woman who had written a book on flower arranging. I said 'Oh, no!' but he had been pressured by his publisher to get a signing session in Scotland and, anyway, I reluctantly agreed. I thought there must be a flower-arranging club. There was, and I found that the secretary was a Mrs Fraser. I telephoned this Mrs Fraser and asked if I could possibly have a list of the members. I offered to send them an invitation inviting them to come and meet this author. They would get a cup of coffee, so they could chat to this woman and she would even do a wee demonstration. Mrs Fraser said, 'I cannot give you my members' names for commercial purposes – you are just trying to sell books', and she put down the phone. Two minutes later, I got a call from the councillor, Graeme Fraser – 'Robert, have you just been speaking to my wife?'

'Graeme, I didn't know it was your wife. It was just a Mrs Fraser to me.' 'Right,' he says, 'you are on. You can send the invitations.' Dozens of the members came. I had the invitations printed by a Mr Wilson in Thistle Street Lane – he did all our printing. It was a right old-fashioned printer's shop. It was a shambles: piles of paper, clippings everywhere. That was a very successful signing and we sold a lot of copies of the book – which was the object of the exercise, and Douglas was delighted.

MOVING ON IN THE 1980S

I was now unemployed after leaving Grant Educational, and I spoke to Bill Bauermeister. He would have given me a job, but there was no senior management post available. At that time he was talking about opening a shop at the campus of Heriot–Watt University at Riccarton. He showed me plans and what not, and the implication was that if it ever happened then I would have the job. Then I got a telephone call from Andrew White and Sons, the printers in Easter Road, to say that there was a chap, Allan Cole Hamilton, that always wanted bookshops and would I be interested in speaking to him. He owned Tubular Scaffolding Limited latterly. and one or two other things. He was one of the high heid yins at the Clydesdale Bank. So we actually bought from Grant's the Union Street shop and the Stirling shop. We called the Glasgow shop the Thistle Bookshop, and a year or so later we opened shops in St Andrews and Perth. We were general booksellers carrying a lot of paperbacks. We were doing fine. I don't think I was unemployed for long – maybe a week in 1982. I was there for four years, until 1986, and it was then my job was questioned. 'What do you do, Robert?' 'I make you a lot of money.' Yes, if I wanted to play golf, I went and played golf – I make no bones about it. What I did basically was to appear every day at some of the shops or all of the shops. I ran stock from one to another, and I went over the order books. I said: 'Don't get too much of that. I will get some from Glasgow.' I moved stuff around and dealt with the publishers, who were my friends. I handled anything awkward, like trying to send stuff back. I could phone and say 'Come on – I will buy you a whisky'. Anyway, it was decided that the two owners could do it on their own, and what I did was dead easy. It *was* dead easy – but then I had been doing it for thirty years. I got the heave. Thank you very much for starting the business; it is doing very well; goodbye! – and that was that. It went into liquidation shortly afterwards. They were nice people, but there is more to bookselling than selling beans. But that was that.

I decided that I was not going to work for anybody else, and I bought a van. I had been an electrician at one stage. I developed a simple burglar alarm in my head. I approached the police, and they recommended me everywhere. Now if you look around Edinburgh, wherever you see a white box with a big 'H' on it, that is my alarm system. I went back to being an electrician, turning full circle after forty years. The book trade had changed, and latterly we were getting people in who had sold beans or soap and knew nothing about what they were selling. In the old days, we had the likes of Norman Parkinson, Graham Fraser and Jimmy Glover. The camaraderie between the book reps went, because you got young salesmen coming in who were given targets, as I had been given targets latterly that I ignored. But these guys were quite insistent, and they were obviously on commission. As a rep you were paid a salary, but latterly it was commission-orientated, to push the sales and push the books; whereas before, we were friends with the publishers, the reps and other booksellers.

It was a nice gentlemanly existence, and bookshops seemed to be able to make a profit without trying too hard. If we did things right, if we bought the right books and displayed them properly, we could sell them. Because we could sell them, we could make a profit, and it wasn't too difficult. It got pretty cut-throat later on, but I think that is the same in many businesses – it is not something peculiar to the book trade. But us old guys did not like it.

Margaret Squires

MARKET TRADER TO BOOKSELLER

The idea for the Quarto Bookshop was sown when Gillian Stone and Pat Hunter met each other in 1969 at an auction in St Andrews and said, 'Where do all the books go, and why isn't there a secondhand bookshop in St Andrews?' There had been a secondhand bookshop that had been run by somebody who was a Japanese prisoner of war, who apparently was not very customer-friendly, but it had closed sometime before we arrived. When we got to St Andrews, I believe there was only one other bookshop in Fife, let alone St Andrews. So Pat said to Gillian, or Gillian said to Pat, 'Let's start one!' Then they began getting cold feet and wondering how they could set about it. Gillian discovered that the statutes of the market meant that anybody could set up a stall in the market, that it was not just fruit and veg people, so that seemed as good a way of testing the water as any. They started thinking about how to get the books to the markets, as Gillian could drive but didn't have a car, and Pat couldn't drive but did live in town with a large pram. So Pat phoned me up and said did I know anybody who could drive. I was ripe for the plucking, because I'd had a tremendous battle with Jean, my daughter, that day – she'd wanted to bring a duck home from the Kinness Burn and had screamed all the

137

way home. When I'd tried to get her to stop crying, she had demanded the right handkerchief for the right day – having had Monday, Tuesday, Wednesday, Thursday and Friday handkerchiefs – and when I'd thrown a handkerchief at her, she said, 'This isn't my Wednesday handkerchief!' I thought, 'I will murder this child if I don't get out of the house sometimes', so when asked if I knew someone who could drive, I just said, 'Yes, me!' We didn't really know each other very well. I had known Pat for about six months because she was the wife of one of my husband's colleagues in the philosophy department at the university, and Gillian and she had met at the auction.

We started accumulating books from auction and then we put a notice in the newspaper, saying that we were in the business of buying books. We bought books from one or two students who needed cash and then we just set up in the market. At the end of day one, we went back to Gillian's house and tipped all the money out of this leather purse that we wore round our belt (or whoever was in charge did), and said, 'Now what?' And I think I said, 'We can't just divide it up; we've got to keep some to spend on more books, and we really need to account for it because the tax man might be interested one day.' I became the accountant, really. We did this for a year. It was quite hard work, and it was also extremely cold and I was pregnant again, and carting books didn't seem like a terribly good idea. But we had made quite a bit of money. When we first set up in the market, this professor's wife swept past us and said, 'What a good idea! Which charity is it going to?' And when we said 'us', she thought that was letting the university down, that university wives should not be in commerce.

THE QUARTO BOOKSHOP

Gillian heard that there was a shop vacant that was run by a trust. In retrospect, we know why we got it. It was because a) they didn't want to tread on anyone else's toes – all the people who were on the trust were in business and they didn't want to set up somebody, or be accused of setting up somebody, in competition with somebody else they might know – and b) it wasn't going to be used for long because the lawyer who was in charge of the trust was busy accumulating properties all round with a view that a supermarket would build on the site. So, we had a site in South Street, 183 South Street, for five years at a rent of £60 a year, during which time Gillian left to go down to Devon with her husband, because he got a job down there. Jenny Hopgood came in to replace her (Jenny Green as she was then), and she brought in the new books side of the business. She joined us largely because she'd had unfortunate experiences working in her previous bookshop in Bell Street in St Andrews, the Paperback Bookshop. Her first boss had been a manic-depressive, and in his manic phase he had gone out and spent all the turnover, I think on a fast car, and then in the depressive stage which followed, when people started asking for money, he'd gone into the attic and threatened to throw himself out of a window, leaving Jenny below to run the shop and phone his mother. Then the shop was taken over by a guy who had worked for Robert Maxwell and had had himself unfortunate experiences with Maxwell. He was an alcoholic, and so he had a tendency to drink all the profits. Jenny decided then she was fed up with fending off people who wanted money and fending off customers who wondered why their books hadn't arrived. Answer: because her bosses couldn't afford to pay for them. She decided she wanted to be in charge, or at least have more control of her life. So she came along to us and asked if she could join in, and we thought it would be a good idea.

We shelved the bookshop in South Street ourselves; there were shelves left over from when it was a wool shop, but some of them weren't particularly good, so we got a local joiner to put shelves in. We didn't pay ourselves for about the first two years: we couldn't afford to. We just put all the money back in. But we did have an employee in the second year, a midwife who was putting her husband through St Andrews University and needed the extra cash. Gillian and Pat did most of the buying to start with, because I'd got two small children. I'd got out of actually moving into the shop, because David was born the day they moved in. In 1969 I was thirty and Pat was forty and Gillian was forty-five, I think. Jenny, who came along two years later, is three years older than me. I did Saturday afternoons, because that was the day they wanted to be with their families, who were school age, and as mine were pre-school, Roger looked after them in the afternoon and I did the accounts. That's all I did, and when Gillian went Jenny came in and took over her slots.

BUYING THE STOCK
Again, that's all I did for quite a while. I did go out and buy with Pat, when Gillian left. I remember going to a minister's house, probably a year after Gillian left, and we had Lucy and David with us, who were probably about two and four, and we had to keep them under control some-how. Ministers are terrible snatchers-back. You go along the shelves, and they suddenly spot something that you've already thought that you wanted and snatch it back and

say, 'No, no, no, no – not that one!' and so you're having to subtract as well as add as you go along. At that stage we used to clear. People said: 'Will you clear?' and we used to. A lot of books we got because people were leaving their houses, and we said we would clear. We'd often divide them into two piles and say: 'These we want and we'll pay you for – these we'll remove if you don't want them, but we'll put them into a charity shop or into a skip because they're not worth anything.' On one particular occasion Pat had bought *The World Pulpit* in something like forty volumes. I didn't want it. I said, 'Is this in or out?' She said, 'It's in.' I tried to push it under his kitchen table, but she spotted it and carried it out. It never sold in the Quarto, and then it went and lived in a shed we bought next to the Quarto in what had used to be a betting shop that had come up for sale. When we moved from South Street to Golf Place I wanted to throw it away, but Pat rescued it and took it up to her house. Then, when Pat finally left – she was extremely honest: she'd written 'P. Borrows' in all the books she'd borrowed from the shop and had taken home to read – there was this huge heap of 'P. Borrows', including *The World Pulpit.* I gave it to the Labour party jumble sale and they couldn't sell it, so they threw it away, and the bin men rescued it and tried to sell it back to me, so that it had this horrible boomerang effect.

It's always tricky going into houses, because the books there have sometimes belonged to someone who has died or, alternatively, it's an unwilling parting; if the person there is the owner of the books, it's often because they're moving to a smaller premises. Very often the husband becomes ill before the wife, and the husband doesn't really want to part with his books, and the wife has just had enough so far as looking after all this huge collection.

There was once a time when we went across to Dundee and bought this guy's books, including all his library of cricket books that he'd obviously loved, and he just went and locked himself into the house. All we saw was this pale, drawn face looking out of the windows as we left. Again, I was summoned to buy someone's collection, including his collection of John Buchan. It was absolutely patent to me that he didn't want to part with his collection of John Buchan. His wife wanted him to part with it. I just said, 'You know, it does seem a pity to break up a collection, and maybe it should all stay here for a little while longer.' I don't think his wife thanked me for that, but that's what happened.

Pat and Jenny and I carried on until Pat left in 1976. Jenny and I had quite a serious discussion about whether we should carry on or not, because we always regarded Pat as the expert. The problem with Pat was always she really wanted to have a bookshop because she wanted lots of books to read, and we had great difficulty in making her price them so that we could sell them, because basically she wanted to have first shot at them. So we'd strike these bargains that she could have first shot at choosing holiday times, if she would price so many books before she went away. Jenny and I were horrible to her once, because we did say that two partners couldn't go away simultaneously – because it was just too difficult to run the shop with only one person, though we actually did have extra staff by then. Pat's husband was one of these people who like to do things at the last minute and be spontaneous. We were going away the first week in July. We had booked it for ages. Geoffrey, her husband, just said to Pat: 'By the way, I've lent our house to these Americans for the first fortnight in July, and so we are going away.' We told Pat she couldn't go away – that she could stay in my house, but not bring her incontinent dog into my house. If she wanted to be with the incontinent dog, she would have to camp in the shop garden. What an appalling thing to do to somebody! But we did. She eventually camped in my garden – well, the incontinent dog lived in a tent in the garden, and Pat lived in my house.

Pat's father was self-taught and was a village schoolmaster, basically, but he wrote the standard work on enclosures. He was a tremendous antiquarian. Tait was her maiden name. Pat had grown up living and breathing books, and we assumed that she knew all about them, and so we had to more or less say, 'Tell us how you do it, Pat' before she left. We knew she looked up book auction records and things like that. There was no internet or anything then. You could look up books in other people's catalogues. Apart from that, it was 'feel', which Pat had and which neither of us had. I had to develop it – rapidly, when she left. I think you develop it by watching other people. Golf books are a prime example of this. You look at a golf book and you think, 'If I were a golfer, would I be interested in this?' I'm not very good at getting the mindset of people so different from me, but you find out what golfers collect, what golfers rate, and then after that it becomes instinctive. You look at a fishing book and you think, 'If this were a golf book, what would it go for?' You have to extend into other subjects. It is much easier in a way now, but there are still some things that escape me because I don't think anybody could rate them, so I don't bother to find out. Then somebody will say, 'Oh, but this is . . .'; 'Oh, I got a tremendous bargain off you once, because . . .' That does happen – of course it happens. You can't win them all, you can't know everything, you just have to hope that you stay in business.

I'm sure that these days people are made to write business plans and stick to them. Well, we didn't have a business plan, and people sometimes say, 'How do you assess things?' And I say, 'Well, I stop buying when the storeroom is full or I run out of money, and I start buying when there's space on the shelves or I've got money.' The textbooks side of the business is a different thing alto-gether. We really only got into that gradually over the years. That's just fairly routine, fairly mundane – you hope you build better and better contacts through the university; try to find out if people are going to drop things next year, but they often don't know before May, when you buy them. Our bread and butter is student textbooks. When we first started, we were much more secondhand and anti-quarian – we might have the odd student textbook, but what veered us a little bit toward that was when we bought the bankrupt stock from Jenny's employer. We wanted to go in and make an offer for it. We did go in, we made an offer for it and the accountant said: 'Pooh-pooh! We will do better in Edinburgh, because Edinburgh is a bigger place.' They turned down our offer, and we came over to Edinburgh to the auction at Dowell's, which was before Philip's, which was the predecessor of Bonham's, and watched things going for pence that we would have paid pounds for. Pat and Jenny went, and hauled back all these textbooks that were tailor-made for St Andrews University, because they had been set there. We bought boxes full of organic chemistry books at 50p. per box. Really, I think that that was what enabled us to get money behind us and have a deposit for the shop when eventually we were chucked out of our first premises, because we were *chucked* out – we really were!

The Golf Place Quarto

The trust had finally lined up the properties, or people's leases had fallen through, and so these four shops were all ready for a supermarket to be built, within the conservation area, within thirty yards of the West Port – absolutely ridiculous: no parking. But that's what they wanted to do, and that's where the supermarket wanted to be. We raised the town against them; we went to umpteen planning meetings and started umpteen petitions. I'd say it was a draw, in a way, in that they didn't get their planning permission, but they were so mad at us that they wouldn't renew our lease. We had to look for something else, and the only something else at the time was premises to buy. So we bought the shop in Golf Place, by a margin of £40, because it was Jenny's fortieth birthday and she said, 'Everyone puts in round numbers; let's just overdo it a bit.' It cost us £12,040. At the last valuation it was something like £125,000. The premises in Golf Place were very similar in size, and the interesting thing was that as we carted books down, sales in the original shop didn't go down. I thought they would. But people, when they see things in cardboard boxes, descend like vultures – they think there are things in there that other people mightn't have seen, even though they were being packed in rather than packed out. We advertised for a strong student to help us move, and then I forgot all about it until this guy turned up at the desk, beating his chest, going, 'Me . . . strong . . . student!' I thought 'God!' 'Yeah,' he said, 'you wanted someone to help you move.' I said, 'Yes, yes, right – I'd forgotten about that'. Alan carried everything – this one, strong student. I drove and he carried and Pat shelved and Jenny unshelved, but it took us quite a while to do it, and meanwhile the shop in South Street stayed open. Mr Eddie the joiner took the shelves out of the old shop and put them into the new shop and we had one or two purpose-built shelves. All sorts of things reappeared in the old shop when we moved, because Lucy, Pat's daughter, used to come and be dropped off with Pat from nursery school. She always used to be desperately hungry, but Pat would say, 'You can't have anything because you won't eat your lunch.' So Lucy would promise she would eat her lunch if only she could have a sausage roll, but halfway though the sausage roll she began to think, 'I'm getting quite full here.' So we found about seven sausage rolls in bags parked behind Theology, which Lucy had deposited, aged four.

We moved down to Golf Place in 1974, and we just opened without a formal ceremony – we missed a trick there. This woman came and banged on the door, desperate to get a particular book for a birthday present, and so the first book we ever sold was called *Sex after Forty*! Which she wanted to give to her boyfriend, I presume. We'd always sold golf books before then, but going down to Golf Place made us realise we had to specialise, and do more golf books. It was just the number of golfers passing by; when you looked at the floor, it was pitted with spikes. The shop previously had been a sweetie shop and tobacconist. Pat said, 'What on earth did this?' and Mrs Morris said, 'Golf spikes', and Pat said, 'Well, I'm not letting golfers in when it's a book shop, then.' Jenny said, 'Yes, we are. We've got to find something to sell them given that many come in.' So that was the start of specialising in new golf books as well as secondhand. Really it's a just a question of evolving to fit what your customers are going to want, because we lost all the people going to the supermarket and coming back and picking up a book on the way. We still kept students, who were prepared to go where textbooks were.

Jenny and I bought Pat out in 1976. Jenny's extremely organised and efficient. She always wants to know what is happening. We had staff by then. To start with, we had Betty Mayo and Pauline Grant. Betty left us when she had to take on more family responsibilities. Pauline moved to the Borders. We got in Pat Riedi, who later took over the new books from Jenny. I then bought Jenny out – so I've done nothing but buy out partners. I must have finished buying Jenny out about eight years ago. Then I could keep some of the money myself. I do the secondhand buying. I have done so since Pat left and Jenny looked after the new side. Jenny came with me occasionally to do second-hand buying; when it was a big house or something like that, we needed two people to have a look at it. We really were mad one time, because we discovered that someone had offered to sell his entire lovely collection of Tayside books to a friend at whatever the Quarto offered plus 10 per cent. We'd gone, and we'd spent hours and hours assessing this collection. We then discovered that it was never going to be ours anyway. Mostly we don't waste time. I don't think I've ever lost a house to somebody who's called in two dealers. I've always made the better offer. I suspect it's because we can also sell 'dross', and people with less space can't sell dross, or don't want to sell dross. Some people say that the ten best books will cover the rest, so you go and look for the ten best books, and you then find what you would sell them for, and you give them that. No – I look at every single book and write it down. So I know exactly what I'm going to sell it for. If I think I'm confident enough that I'm going to get it, I'll put it in pencil inside the book, if the seller doesn't notice what I'm up to. That way I know that I'm going to not do something silly, and I know that I'm going to make a profit.

The other thing is I don't take a computer or anything like that with me. I don't take much, really. I sometimes take *Books in Print* with me to check if something's in print, but I've hardly ever used it – it's just a waste of time. I sometimes up prices, and I sometimes down prices when I look them up, but by and large, swings and roundabouts, I'll end up looking up something like a quarter of the books that I buy these days – that's maybe because I'm getting less confident.

THE INTERNET

I now look them up on the internet, because there are books that I've been shocked at. I bought, the other day, a book called *Royal Gardens*. Only 245 were ever published, a superb book, lots of nice tipped-in pictures, and blow me, there are fifty-five copies on the internet and the cheapest – ex-library, admittedly – is eighteen quid. This is a book that I would have, had I not thought about it, probably tried to sell for £80 – and would never have sold. I look up Addall: it does other things besides books, but it does do books, new books as well as used books. If you put a forward-slash 'used' in, that comes up. So I do check up people's prices. I think it's rather sad; it's putting runners like Jim McMaster out of work. Jim McMaster is also a very astute bookseller as well. In the secondhand world, what one person can buy and does know about will be different from the next, and someone like him can capitalise. Jim has an absolutely amazing retentive memory. I don't know how he does it. People come in with books to sell and they will have printouts from the internet in their books. At that moment when that happens, I say, well, okay, this is from the internet – it's not necessarily the only one on the internet. We could look it up now:

I've got a computer in the shop. I don't sell antiquarian on the internet. I sell stuff that I can't sell in the shop, namely textbooks that have gone off recommended lists. I sell them on Amazon, and I get – for what I consider total rubbish, such as old management texts – a reasonable amount of money. I can at least get my investment back, which I never used to. I would either have to bin these or send them to the Ranfurly library (which dispatches books to the third world), which I now have no way of doing, because the rotary club has stopped sending lorry-loads down. The bookshop stock is valued at £56,000, at cost, which is worrying because you think, 'I'll not get that back in a hurry.' I wouldn't have to now; I would just cart it home and sell it gradually over the internet.

CUSTOMERS

Most of the customers of the Quarto who are at all academic probably know far more than I do about their own particular subject. There's a guy at the moment who is researching a book. He was going to write a book on Jacobite clothes, but he realised that he doesn't know enough about how clothes degrade, what to do scientifically to get back from the fragments as they are now to what they would have been, so he's switched to writing about the Jacobite army. He wants everything Jacobite. I recognise suitable stuff to send him, which he's usually quite pleased with. He's prepared to buy things even in appalling condition, just so he can read them, which really appeals to me because I don't think books ought to be worshipped, I think they ought to be read. He's an interesting bloke. Some of the staff of the university are interesting. Bob Prescott comes and buys anything that the fisheries museum in Anstruther hasn't got, because he's on the board of that. And he will buy anything that's useful about maritime archaeology. Colin Martin, who's also into maritime archaeology, once bought a book from us that apparently saved him hours and days and weeks and months in dismantling this ship they had found, because this particular book showed how it was put together.

The trouble is that, behind the counter, you don't really have an awful lot of time to talk to people about their specialities. The hours are ten till half past five. We never used to have lunch hour or Sundays. We do now, largely because we had an American student who came and said: 'I notice you don't work lunch hours or Sundays, I think you could do well. Let me do them as an experiment, you don't have to pay me unless they do work out.' And they did, and we paid him, and that means we now have to continue doing it, because he left quite a while ago. His mum had run off with his trust fund. Besides working for us, he also caddied, and he used to get some appalling customers. He got a first in mediaeval history, so he did well. Our Saturday people do go on to do good things. Nick got a first despite working all the lunch hours and Sunday; he was a debater as well, and went on to be a barrister, and worked in Michael Mansfield's chambers, which were his great ambition, and now he works in the human rights practice in Manchester – the only human rights practice in the north of England. Will went on to Oxford, where he got the best degree in English of his year; he is now a lecturer there. Eliza is lecturing. Jessie went on to work for Claire Short and [became] one of the youngest councillors in London.

We launched Anna Crowe's book here. Anna works for me and is also the artistic director of *Stanza*. She's written a book called *Skating out of the House* [1997] and is just launching another one shortly, called *A Secret History of Rhubarb* [2004]. Mariscat Press is publishing it. Anna was told on good authority that if you ask people to book launches, between 25 and 30 per cent of people you ask come. Well, Anna is so nice and people like her so much she asked something like ninety people and seventy came. There just wasn't room for them in the shop; we had to push them out in the garden at the back; and they kept trying to get back in to hear her read. We've had golf launches, one of which was a total dead loss, because Sid Matthew wanted to launch his book about Bobby Jones in the Quarto in February. I said February was not a good time of year to launch any golf book. But he said he wanted it done then; he'd already launched it in America. So I said, 'Okay.' I put a lot of publicity round in the golf clubs and in the *Citizen*, and I recommended the best time to do it would be one o'clock, when golfers could possibly get off for lunch. At five to one, Sid and his publisher slunk into the shop and said they'd just been invited out to lunch at the R and A [Royal and Ancient] and they'd be back soon. They reappeared at four o'clock, and we weren't best pleased with them. I phoned up his English publisher and said: 'You are a really nice person – what are you doing involved with people like this?' He sent me this huge bunch of flowers, and I thought, 'That's all very well.' Sid came back into the shop two years later and said to Pat, 'Is Margaret still mad at me?' Pat said, 'Well, I think there are some fences that could do with mending' – and I got another huge bunch of flowers. We launched Ian Nalder's *Scotland's Golf in Days of Steam*. It's a good book for golf buffs and for steam buffs, so it scores twice over since there are lots of both of them.

Sid Scroggie came from Dundee. He wrote a book

called *The Cairngorms, Seen and Unseen* [1989]. He is a Dundee character. He was blown up in Monte Cassino in the Second World War and lost eyes and a leg. When he came back, he was fed up not going hill-walking, so he put an advert in the *Courier* saying: 'Blind man wants somebody to take him to the hills.' The guy from the advertising department answered it – so it never actually got into the newspaper – and said, 'I'll take you.' They got ever more ambitious, and they ended up camping in the Lairig Ghru or somewhere. This advertising guy, in the middle of the night, reached up and felt this wooden object and thought, 'What the hell is this?' and Sid said, 'Oh, that's my leg.' He thought he was taking a blind man, not a blind man with one leg. Anyway, Sid used to come to the Quarto and always provided us with great entertainment.

It does get a bit quieter in the summer, despite the tourists. Our real boom is at the beginning of September, when the students come back, and this coincides with the Autumn Medal. There are lots of golfers around still in September. Then there's this long-drawn-out ebbing-away of trade. We don't have Christmas trade much. People don't give paperbacks, which we mostly sell. We sell some golf books as Christmas presents, but secondhand books mostly don't sell for Christmas presents. Then we get all the people who've left St Andrews and come back to their elderly parents coming in between Christmas and New Year. They've often been in as younger people, and redis-cover us, and they come back in, and we get quite a good Christmas to New Year period. Then it goes quiet again, because students are really away until February now. It's very peculiar, this new semester thing. They used to be back in January, but now it's not until February. February is excellent, March is not too bad. We stock-take as soon as the students go on holiday. We stock-take, and that's usually quite quiet, and then Easter peps it up again, usually. May is normally quite good, because we're buying in books for the following year, and some students who think they know what's going to be on the course for next year come and purchase then. We also get the tourist buses starting around April as well. There's one bloke who always brings in his small tour group. He was a Fifer, and in fact he ran the Newburgh Festival, and he often brings groups of Americans. They're into clans and tartans – not just the general stuff, they want their own particular clan history. They know a lot of history. It's not just: 'My name's MacKenzie, I must be related to all the MacKenzies in the world.'

The Quarto Bookshop closed in 2006.